AN ADAPTED CLASSIC

Romeo and Juliet

William Shakespeare

GLOBE FEARON

Pearson Learning Group

Adapter: Arvin Casas
Project Editor: Kristen Shepos-Salvatore
Editorial Supervisor: Cary Pepper
Editorial Assistant: Kathleen Kennedy
Production Editor: Alan Dalgleish
Marketing Manager: Sandra Hutchison
Art Supervision: Patricia Smythe
Electronic Page Production: Luc Van Meerbeek
Cover and Interior Illustrator: James McDaniel

ISBN 0-8359-1845-9
Printed in the United States of America

22 23 24 25 26 27 28 29 30 V036 15 14 13

Globe
Fearon

Pearson Learning Group

1-800-321-3106
www.pearsonlearning.com

CONTENTS

About the Author iv

Adapter's Note v

Preface v

Historical Background vi

Cast of Characters........................... viii

Act 1

    Scene 1.. 1

    Scene 2.. 6

    Scene 3....................................... 10

    Scene 4....................................... 12

    Scene 5....................................... 14

Act 2

    Scene 1....................................... 21

    Scene 2....................................... 22

    Scene 3....................................... 28

    Scene 4....................................... 30

    Scene 5....................................... 35

    Scene 6....................................... 37

Act 3

    Scene 1....................................... 39

    Scene 2....................................... 45

    Scene 3....................................... 48

    Scene 4....................................... 52

    Scene 5....................................... 53

Act 4

    Scene 1....................................... 60

    Scene 2....................................... 63

    Scene 3....................................... 65

    Scene 4....................................... 68

    Scene 5....................................... 69

Act 5

    Scene 1....................................... 73

    Scene 2....................................... 75

    Scene 3....................................... 76

Summary of the Play........................... 89

Reviewing Your Reading 93

ABOUT THE AUTHOR

There are many things we do not know for certain about William Shakespeare. It is believed he was born on April 26, 1564. He grew up in Stratford upon Avon, a small town in England. He married Anne Hathaway in 1582, when he was 18. They had three children, two girls and one boy. Shakespeare went to London, where he became successful as an actor, a playwright, and a poet. He belonged to a group of actors called The King's Men, who performed his plays. In 1599, The King's Men built a theater, which they named the Globe. The Globe became one of the best-known theaters in London. Shakespeare's plays were also performed at court, for Queen Elizabeth I and King James I. Shakespeare retired from the theater around 1613. He returned to Stratford, where he bought a house and land. William Shakespeare died on April 23, 1616. He is buried in Stratford.

Who really wrote Shakespeare's plays is one of literature's great mysteries. Some people say that one man could not have written so many excellent plays. Some people think that if one man did write them, it was not Shakespeare, because they believe he was poorly educated. Other people say he did write the plays that bear his name, and consider William Shakespeare the world's greatest playwright.

ADAPTER'S NOTE

This is an adapted version of *Romeo and Juliet*. We have changed much of the form and language of the original. Special care has been taken, however, to keep the feel and flavor of Shakespeare. Although the poetry has been altered, the poetic images remain. The story has not been changed.

PREFACE

Romeo and Juliet is a popular play with young people as well as adults. Over the years, the play has intrigued writers, poets, musicians, and other artists. It has been performed as Hollywood films and Broadway musicals.

The story of *Romeo and Juliet* originally came from popular Italian poems and French novels. Though the story was not new, Shakespeare used it in a new way. Playwrights used to set their stories in ancient Greece and Rome. This was a style and a fashion of Shakespeare's time. Many of his other plays are like this. But people found it hard to relate to Roman emperors and Greek gods. That is why Shakespeare used an everyday story about a boy and a girl and their forbidden love for his play. The fact that *Romeo and Juliet* is still popular today shows how clever Shakespeare was to do this.

The appeal of *Romeo and Juliet* is timeless. Young people will always fall in love. Parents will always seem heartless. The world will always seem cruel. As long as this is so, *Romeo and Juliet* will continue to be popular.

HISTORICAL BACKGROUND

Shakespeare's most productive years were during what is called the Elizabethan Age in England. During the years of Elizabeth I's reign (1558–1603), theatrical drama was very important. This period is also known as the English Renaissance. London's first public theater was built in 1576 by James Burbage. It was so popular that by 1585 a second playhouse was being used.

Shakespeare's London was a busy medieval city. It was the center of England's social, business, and intellectual life. It was the only city in England that was fully under the influence of the Renaissance (the flowering of art and culture in Italy, France, and Spain). Most of the printing and publishing in England was done in London. In England, theaters for the public performance of drama were found only in London. London, in short, was the heart of England. In the sense that he pumped new life into London's cultural scene, Shakespeare was the heart of London.

Elizabethan Theater

Theaters in Shakespeare's time were designed very differently from modern theaters. The stage jutted out into the audience. It took up the space now used by the first few rows of seats. This stage had no curtain to be raised, lowered, or opened. There were hardly any stage props. Sets were very simple. In fact, the audience had to use their imagination a great deal. For them, the same set might have to work as a street scene or a ballroom scene.

The rear of the stage had a small curtained area. This could be used as an inner room, a tomb, or a prison. There were balconies on the sides of the stage. These were used for upper decks of ships, balconies of houses, and prison windows.

When theaters were not available, plays were performed in public places, such as inns and taverns. This is one reason Elizabethan plays had so many speeches that could be delivered in loud voices. The playwright had to make sure the audience could hear everything.

These were just some of the physical differences between Elizabethan theater and today's theater. There was also another important difference. Women were not allowed to act. All parts were played by men. Most women's roles were played by boys. They were often recruited from the boys' choirs in London churches.

CAST OF CHARACTERS

THE HOUSE OF MONTAGUE

MONTAGUE
Romeo's father and head of the House

LADY MONTAGUE
Montague's wife and Romeo's mother

ROMEO
Montague's only son

BENVOLIO
Cousin and friend of Romeo

BALTHASAR
Romeo's servant

ABRAHAM
Servant of the House of Montague

THE HOUSE OF CAPULET

CAPULET
Juliet's father and head of the House

LADY CAPULET
Capulet's wife and Juliet's mother

JULIET
Capulet's only daughter

TYBALT
Juliet's cousin

COUSIN CAPULET
An old man, cousin of Capulet

NURSE
Juliet's nurse and companion

SAMPSON
Servant of the House of Capulet

GREGORY
Servant of the House of Capulet

PETER
> A servant of Juliet's nurse

PRINCE ESCALUS
> Prince of Verona

PARIS
> A young nobleman, relative of the Prince

MERCUTIO
> Relative of the Prince, and friend of Romeo

PARIS'S SERVANT

FRIAR LAWRENCE
> A Franciscan monk and Romeo's friend

FRIAR JOHN
> Another monk

A DRUGGIST

THREE MUSICIANS

CITIZENS OF VERONA

MEN AND WOMEN FROM BOTH HOUSES

MASKERS

TORCHBEARERS

WATCHMEN

SERVANTS AND ATTENDANTS

Act 1

Scene 1

Verona. A public place. SAMPSON *and* GREGORY, *of the House of Capulet, enter. They are armed with swords.*

SAMPSON: Gregory, on my word, I will go to the wall with any dog Montague.

GREGORY: The quarrel is between our masters and us, their servants.

SAMPSON: I'll fight them all, the men and the maidens too.

GREGORY: Even the women? Well, draw your sword! Here come two Montagues.

SAMPSON: My weapon is already ready. Pick a fight. I will back you up.

GREGORY: How? By turning your back and running?

SAMPSON: Don't be afraid of them.

GREGORY: I'm more afraid of you!

SAMPSON: Let's keep the law on our side. Let them start something.

GREGORY: I'll frown at them as they pass by.

SAMPSON: I will bite my thumb and insult them.
Let's see how they take that.

(ABRAHAM *and* BALTHASAR *enter.*)

ABRAHAM: Do you bite your thumb at us, sir?

SAMPSON: I am biting my thumb, sir.

ABRAHAM: Are you biting it at us, sir?

SAMPSON (*aside to* GREGORY): Is the law on our side, if I say yes?

GREGORY: No.

SAMPSON: No, sir, I do not bite my thumb at you, sir. But I am biting my thumb.

GREGORY: Do you want to start a fight, sir?

ABRAHAM: A fight, sir! No.

SAMPSON: But if you do, I'll fight you. I serve as good a man as you do.

ABRAHAM: No, I serve better.

SAMPSON: Draw!

(*They fight.* BENVOLIO *enters.*)

BENVOLIO: Part, fools! You don't know what you're doing. (*He beats down their swords.*)

(TYBALT *enters.*)

TYBALT: So! Are you one of these fools too?
    Turn around Benvolio,
    And look upon your death.

BENVOLIO: I'm trying to stop them.
    Put up your sword,
    Or use it to stop these men with me.

TYBALT: You talk of peace! I hate the word,
    As I hate hell, all Montagues, and you.
    Come on, coward!

(*They fight. Enter, several of both houses, who join the fray. Then enter* CITIZENS, *with clubs.*)

CITIZENS: Down with the Capulets!
    Down with the Montagues!

(CAPULET *enters, in his gown, with* LADY CAPULET.)

CAPULET: What noise is this? Give me my long sword!

LADY CAPULET: A crutch, you mean. Why a sword?

CAPULET: My sword, I say! Old Montague is coming.
　　He's waving his blade to spite me.

(MONTAGUE *enters with* LADY MONTAGUE.)

MONTAGUE: You villain Capulet. Wife! Let me go!

LADY MONTAGUE: No, not one foot against your foe.

(PRINCE ESCALUS *enters with attendants.*)

PRINCE: Rebellious subjects, enemies to peace.
　　You beasts who put out the fires of anger with blood!
　　Throw your weapons to the ground,
　　And hear the sentence of your angry prince.
　　Three fights, started by you,
　　Old Capulet and Montague,
　　Have disturbed the quiet streets of Verona.
　　If any of you ever does so again,
　　You shall pay with your lives for breaking the peace.
　　You, Capulet, come along with me.
　　Montague, see me this afternoon.
　　We will discuss this case, at our common judgment
　　　　place.
　　Once more, on pain of death, all men depart.

(*Exit* ALL *but* MONTAGUE, LADY MONTAGUE, *and*
BENVOLIO.)

MONTAGUE: Who started up this old quarrel?
　　Speak nephew, were you there when it began?

BENVOLIO: The servants of your enemy,
　　And yours, were fighting when I approached.

I drew my sword to part them, but the fiery Tybalt,
With his sword ready, shouted insults at me
And slashed his weapon in the wind.
While we were swapping thrusts and blows,
More came, fighting on both sides,
Till the prince came, who stopped us all.

LADY MONTAGUE: Where is Romeo? Have you seen him
today?
I am glad he was not here.

BENVOLIO: Madam, an hour before the sun
Peered from the golden window of the east,
My troubled mind made me go for a walk.
I saw your son in a grove of sycamores
And I walked over to him.
Hearing me, he fled and hid in the woods.
I understood his need to be alone,
So I gladly let him be.

MONTAGUE: Many a morning has he been seen there,
Adding his tears to the fresh morning dew,
Clouding the sky with his deep sighs.
As soon as the cheerful sun begins to rise,
My son runs home, away from the light,
Locking himself in his room, shutting his window,
Locking out the daylight.
He lives in his own artificial night.

BENVOLIO: My noble uncle, do you know the cause?

MONTAGUE: No, and he will not tell me.
Romeo keeps his secrets to himself.
I wish we knew from where his sorrows grow.
We would willingly cure him of them, you know.

BENVOLIO: Here he comes. If you'll please step aside,
I'll learn his problem. I won't be denied.

MONTAGUE: Come, madam, let's leave.

(*He exits with* LADY MONTAGUE. ROMEO *enters.*)

BENVOLIO: Good morning, cousin.

ROMEO: Is it morning?

BENVOLIO: The clock just struck nine.

ROMEO: Ah me! Sad hours seem long.
　　Was that my father who left here so fast?

BENVOLIO: Yes. What sadness makes Romeo's hours long?

ROMEO: I'm out of her favor, of the one I love.

BENVOLIO: Alas that love, so gentle in appearance,
　　Should make us feel so bad!

ROMEO: Oh my! What fight was here?
　　Don't tell me, for I have heard it all.
　　There is much to do with hate here, but more with
　　　love.
　　Oh fighting love! Oh loving hate!
　　This love I feel, feels no love in this.
　　Do you laugh at me?

BENVOLIO: No, I weep at your heart's suffering.

ROMEO: Such is love. Love is a smoke of sighs;
　　A fire sparkling in lovers' eyes;
　　A sea nourished with lovers' tears.
　　It is a madness roaring in a wise man's ears.
　　Farewell.

BENVOLIO: Wait! I will go along with you.

ROMEO: I have lost myself. I am not here.
　　This is not Romeo. He's somewhere else.

BENVOLIO: Tell me, who is it that you love?

ROMEO: Cousin, I love a woman.

BENVOLIO: I guessed so, when I guessed you loved.

ROMEO: But she'll not be hit with Cupid's arrow.
She lives unharmed from Love's bow.
She will not fall to love's attack,
My longing eyes, or saint-seducing gold.
She is rich in beauty. What a shame
That her treasure will die with her.

BENVOLIO: She has sworn that she will never love?

ROMEO: She has.
She has sworn to live without love,
And I die from that vow.

BENVOLIO: Listen to me, forget her.

ROMEO: That would be like forgetting to think!

BENVOLIO: Free your eyes. Look at other beauties.

ROMEO: A blind man cannot forget his lost sight!
And I can't forget her beauty, try as hard as I might.
Farewell. You cannot teach me to forget.

BENVOLIO: I will, or will die trying yet.

(*They exit.*)

Scene 2

A street. CAPULET, PARIS, *and a* SERVANT *enter.*

CAPULET: Montague, as well as I, must obey the law.
It is not hard for old men to keep the peace.

PARIS: Both of you are honorable men.
It is a pity that you have fought for so long.
But now, sir, what do you say?
May I marry your daughter, Juliet?

CAPULET: As I have said, my child is too young.
She is not even fourteen.

Let two more summers go by. Then she will be ready.

PARIS: Younger girls than she have married.

CAPULET: And those that have are more often ruined.
   The grave has taken all my children but Juliet.
   She is my last joy on earth.
   But you may try to win her heart, Paris.
   My permission is only a part. If she agrees,
   And chooses you, I will agree.
   Tonight I am having a party,
   And I have invited many guests.
   Please come, too.
   Many beautiful women will be there.
   Listen and look, choose the best of them all.
   You may find that my daughter
   May not even be to your liking.

(*He gives the* SERVANT *a piece of paper.*)

   Go invite the people
   Whose names are written there
   Welcome them to my home.

(CAPULET *and* PARIS *exit.*)

SERVANT: Invite the names written here! How? I cannot
   write or read! I must find someone who can.

(ROMEO *and* BENVOLIO *enter.*)

BENVOLIO: Romeo, cheer up! One fire can put out another,
   Just as a larger ache can make you forget a smaller
      pain.
   Take a new girl to your eye,
   And those old sorrows of yours will die.

ROMEO: I cannot. I am a madman for her,
   Shut up in prison, kept without food,

Whipped and tormented.

SERVANT: Excuse me sir. Can you read?

ROMEO: Yes. I can read fortunes. Mine is miserable.

SERVANT: Oh. Can you read anything else?

ROMEO: Let me see your paper. (*He reads*) "Signior
Martino and his wife and daughters. Count Anselme
and his beauteous sisters. Mercutio and his brother
Valentine. Uncle Capulet, his wife and daughters. My
fair niece Rosaline. Livia. Signior Valentio and his
cousin Tybalt."
Quite a guest list! Where are they going?

SERVANT: To supper, at our house.

ROMEO: Whose house?

SERVANT: My master's.

ROMEO: Perhaps I should have asked you that first.

SERVANT: Don't ask, I'll tell you. My master is the great,
rich Capulet. If you're not a Montague, you may
come for a drink as well. Thank you!

(SERVANT *exits.*)

BENVOLIO: That Rosaline, who you love so much,
Will be at Capulet's tonight
With all the other beauties of Verona.
Let's go there and compare her face with the others.
I'll show you that your swan is really a crow.

ROMEO: No one is prettier than Rosaline!
The sun has never seen one like her
Since the world began.

BENVOLIO: You saw her with no one to compare her to.
Tonight, she'll seem less than some I'll show you.

ROMEO: I'll go, no such sights to be shown,
But to rejoice in the beauty of my own.

(*They exit.*)

Scene 3

A room in Capulet's house. LADY CAPULET *and* NURSE *enter.*

LADY CAPULET: Nurse, where's my daughter? Call her.

NURSE: Juliet!

(JULIET *enters.*)

JULIET: Mother, I am here. What do you wish?

LADY CAPULET: Nurse, excuse us please,
We must talk in private. No, wait! You may stay and listen.
Do you know my daughter's age?

NURSE: Yes, I can tell her age up to the hour.

LADY CAPULET: Is she fourteen?

NURSE: I'll bet fourteen of my teeth, though I only have four. But now that I think of it, she's not fourteen. When is the festival of Lammastide[1]?

LADY CAPULET: In about two weeks.

NURSE: Then she will be fourteen.
I can remember it all. It's been eleven years
Since I first took care of her.
Even at that age she could stand by herself.
She could run and waddle all around.

---

1. **Lammastide** August 1; a holiday of thanksgiving to celebrate the wheat harvest

One day she hurt her head. My husband picked
   her up
And said, "Did you fall on your face?
When you're older and smarter
You'll fall backwards, won't you?"
She left crying and said, "Yes."
If I live a thousand years, I will never forget that.

LADY CAPULET: Please, enough of this. Be quiet.

NURSE: It still makes me laugh. She had a huge bump.

JULIET: Please, Nurse, please stop.

NURSE: You were the prettiest baby I ever nursed.
I hope I live long enough to see you married.

LADY CAPULET: That's what I came to talk about.
Tell me, Juliet,
What do you think about marriage?

JULIET: It is an honor I do not dream about.

LADY CAPULET: Well, think of it now.
Here in Verona,
There are mothers younger than you.
I was younger than you are when I had you.
Did you know that the handsome Paris wants to
   marry you?

NURSE: Juliet! What a man! He's perfect!

LADY CAPULET: Tonight he will be at our party.
Look closely at his face. Examine him like a book—
A handsome book that only needs you as a cover.
As his wife, you will share everything he has.
What do you say? Could you love Paris?

JULIET: I'll look at him, if that's all it takes
To love. But I will only look as much as I have to,
Because you want me to.

SERVANT (*enters*): Madam! The guests are here and
supper has been served. Everyone is waiting for you
and Juliet. Please come at once.

LADY CAPULET: We're coming. (SERVANT *exits.*)
Juliet, Paris is waiting for you.

NURSE: Go, Juliet. Happy nights
Will bring you happy days, too.

(ALL *exit.*)

Scene 4

A street. ROMEO, MERCUTIO, BENVOLIO, *with five or six*
Maskers, Torchbearers, and others enter.

ROMEO: Will we say something when we get there?
Or will we sneak in quietly?

BENVOLIO: We don't need to say anything.
Let them take us as they will.
We'll dance a little, then be gone.

ROMEO: Give me a torch to hold. I am in no mood for this.
My heart is so heavy, I will just carry the light.

MERCUTIO: No, Romeo. We want you to dance.

ROMEO: Not me! You have dancing shoes
With graceful soles. I have a soul of lead
That nails me to the ground. I cannot move.

MERCUTIO: You are a lover.
Borrow Cupid's wings and fly.

ROMEO: I am too sore from his arrow
To fly with his feathers.
I am so heavy with love, I sink.

MERCUTIO: Sink? You make love sound heavy
For such a tender thing.

ROMEO: Is love a tender thing? It is too rough.
  It cuts like a thorn.

MERCUTIO: If love is rough with you,
  Be rough with love.
  Cut the thorn that cuts you,
  And beat love down.
  Give me my mask to hide my face.

BENVOLIO: Here we are, knock and enter.
  As soon as we go in, start dancing.

ROMEO: Only a torch for me.
  Let those whose hearts are light,
  Click their heels. As the old proverb says,
  I'll just be a candleholder,
  And look on from the side.

MERCUTIO: Then everyone will notice you.
  We'll pull you out of the mud
  That you're stuck in up to your ears.
  Come on, we're wasting time,
  Like burning lamps during the day.

ROMEO: We mean well in going to this party,
  But it's not smart to go.

MERCUTIO: Why, may one ask?

ROMEO: I dreamed a dream last night.

MERCUTIO: And so did I.

ROMEO: Well, what was yours?

MERCUTIO: That dreamers often lie.

ROMEO: When they are in bed asleep,
  They dream the truth.

MERCUTIO: I see Queen Mab[2] has been with you.

---

2. Mab fairy spirit believed to bring people dreams

She is the Fairy Queen who drives a carriage
Pulled by little creatures across men's noses as they
   sleep.
Her wagon-spokes are made of spiders' legs.
Her driver is a small grey-coated bug.
She gallops every night
Through lovers' brains, making them dream of love.
She gallops over ladies' lips, and they dream of kisses.
This is the very Mab that braids the manes of horses
   in the night,
And tangles your hair in bed.

ROMEO: Enough! Mercutio, Please! Your words say
   nothing.

MERCUTIO: Dreams are the children of a bored brain.
   They are nothing but fantasy,
   Thin as air wherever the wind blows.

BENVOLIO: This wind you talk of
   Has blown us the wrong way.
   Supper is over. We will be late.

ROMEO: I fear we are too early. I have the feeling
   That something bad is hanging in the stars.
   Something will begin at tonight's party,
   That will end my life early. Oh well.
   Fate, or whoever sets my course, direct my sail!
   Let us go, gentlemen.

(*They exit.*)

Scene 5

A hall in Capulet's house. MUSICIANS *stand waiting.*
SERVANTS *enter with napkins.*

FIRST SERVANT: Where's Potpan? He is supposed to help

clear away these plates!

SECOND SERVANT: You can't rely on him or his hands.

FIRST SERVANT: Move these stools. Remove the sideboard,
   and care for the silverware. Go tell the porter to send
   in Susan Grindstone and Nell. (*Exit* SECOND SERVANT.)

(CAPULET, JULIET, *and others of his house enter, meeting
the* GUESTS *and* MASKERS.)

CAPULET: Welcome, gentlemen!
   The ladies without corns on their feet will dance
      with you.
   Ah ha, my ladies! Which of you refuses to dance?
   If you play shy, I'll tell everyone that you have corns!
   Welcome, gentlemen! I remember the days
   When I used to wear a mask
   And whisper in a lady's ear.
   Oh, those days are gone, but you are welcome!
   Come, musicians, play. Make room!
   Dance, girls. (*Music plays, and they dance.*) Servants!
   More light! Move these tables!
   Put out the fire, the room is too hot.
   Ah hello! Please sit, good cousin Capulet!
   You and I are past our dancing days.
   How long is it since you and I were in masks?

COUSIN CAPULET: My word! Thirty years.

CAPULET: What! It hasn't been that long.
   We wore masks at Lucentio's wedding, twenty-five
      years ago.

COUSIN CAPULET: More than that! His son is thirty.

CAPULET: He was only a child two years ago.

ROMEO (*to a* SERVANT): What lady is that
   Who dances with that knight?

SERVANT: I know not, sir.

ROMEO: Oh, she teaches the torches to burn bright!
　　She hangs upon the cheek of night.
　　Her beauty is too rich for earth—she glows!
　　She's like a snowy dove among crows.
　　The song is over. I'll see where she stands.
　　Simply touching her will bless my hands.
　　Did my heart love till now?
　　Not at this sight!
　　For I never saw true beauty till this night.

TYBALT: That voice! I know he is a Montague.
　　Fetch me my sword, boy.
　　How dare that slave come here, with such a happy
　　　face.
　　He mocks us at our own party.
　　By the honor of my kin,
　　I'll strike him dead, and not count it a sin.

CAPULET: Tybalt! Where are you storming off to?

TYBALT: Uncle, a villain Montague, our foe,
　　Has come here in spite
　　To mock us and spoil our party tonight.

CAPULET: Young Romeo is it?

TYBALT: It is he, that villain Romeo.

CAPULET: Calm down. Leave him alone.
　　He looks like a well-behaved gentleman.
　　From what I hear, all of Verona
　　Says he is decent and well-mannered.
　　Not for all the wealth of this town
　　Will I insult him in my own house.
　　Take no note of him.
　　Respect my wishes and stop frowning.
　　Your sour face is wrong for a party.

TYBALT: It fits, when such a villain is a guest.
I won't allow it.

CAPULET: You will allow it! Am I the master here,
Or are you? Stop.
You're going to make a scene
In front of my guests!

TYBALT: Uncle, it is a shame.

CAPULET: Ignore it. My, you are an angry young boy.
Now be quiet.
(*to* SERVANTS) More light, more light!
Everyone, more cheer!

TYBALT: My patience is wearing thin.
It makes my skin crawl. I must leave.

(TYBALT *exits.* ROMEO *goes to* JULIET *and takes her hand.*)

ROMEO: If my hand is unworthy of holding yours,
That holy shrine,
Charge me with this gentle fine:
My lips are like two blushing pilgrims,
Ready to smooth the hand's rough touch
With a tender kiss.

JULIET: Good sir, you do your hands a great wrong.
Is it not palm-to-palm that pilgrims pray?

ROMEO: But pilgrims pray with pilgrims' lips as well.

JULIET: Yes. We must use lips to pray.

ROMEO: Oh then, dear saint, answer my prayer,
And let our lips meet, or I despair. (*They kiss.*)

JULIET: You kiss by the book.[3]

---

3. **You kiss by the book.** Juliet is saying that Romeo kisses
well.

NURSE: Madam, your mother craves a word with you.

(JULIET *exits.*)

ROMEO: Who is her mother?

NURSE: Her mother is the lady of the house.
I nursed the girl you just spoke with.
I tell you, whoever marries her will be rich.

(NURSE *walks away.*)

ROMEO: Is she a Capulet? Oh no!
My life is in the hands of my foe.

BENVOLIO: Let's leave. The party is over.

ROMEO: Ah, so I fear.

CAPULET (*to everyone*): Gentlemen, do not go.
We have refreshments.
You must go?
Why, then, I thank you, honest gentlemen. Good
night.

(ALL *begin to file out except* JULIET *and* NURSE.)

JULIET: Come here, Nurse. Who is that gentleman?

NURSE: The son and heir of old Tiberio.

JULIET: Who is that, now going out the door?

NURSE: That, I think, is young Petrucio.

JULIET: And who is that there, who would not dance?

NURSE: I do not know.

JULIET: Go ask his name.
(NURSE *leaves.*)
If he is married,
A grave will be my wedding bed.

NURSE (*returning*): His name is Romeo,

And a Montague!
The only son of your great enemy.

JULIET: My only love comes from my only hate!
If I'd known earlier! But it is too late!
How awful love is to me,
That I must love my enemy.

NURSE: What are you saying?

JULIET: A rhyme I learned from someone tonight.

(*A voice from offstage calls for* JULIET.)

NURSE: Come, let's go up. The guests have all gone.

(*They exit.*)

Act 2

Scene 1

A lane by the wall of Capulet's orchard. ROMEO *enters.*

ROMEO: How can I leave when my heart is here?
 I must turn around and find my center.

(He climbs the wall, and leaps down behind it.)

*(*BENVOLIO *enters with* MERCUTIO.*)*

BENVOLIO: Romeo! My cousin, Romeo!

MERCUTIO: If he is wise, he has gone home to bed.

BENVOLIO: No, I think he ran this way
 And leaped over this orchard wall.
 Call him, Mercutio.

MERCUTIO: I'll call him with magic words.
 Oh Romeo! Madman! Passion! Lover!
 Appear here in the form of a sigh.
 Say just one rhyme, and I will be satisfied.
 Cry out "Ah me!" or just "love" or "dove."
 Speak now to the goddess of love.
 Say just one fair word for her son Cupid.
 He doesn't hear or stir. He won't move.
 That ape is dead! I must bring him back to life.
 I'll use the magic of his Rosaline.
 By her bright eyes, high forehead, and red lips,
 By her fine foot, straight leg, and all the rest,
 Appear to us now!

BENVOLIO: If he hears you, you will make him angry.

MERCUTIO: No. My spell is fair and honest.

I'm only using Rosaline's name to rile[1] him.

BENVOLIO: Forget it. He is hiding in the trees,
To be alone with the night.
His blind love is best in the dark.

MERCUTIO: If love is blind, how can it hit its target?
He is probably sitting under a tree,
Wishing that his love were the fruit.
Oh Romeo, that she were a pear!
Good night Romeo! I'm going to bed. Shall we go?

BENVOLIO: Let's go. It's useless to look for someone
Who does not want to be found.

(*They exit.*)

Scene 2

Capulet's orchard. ROMEO *enters.*

ROMEO: He laughs at love's scars,
But Mercutio has never felt such a wound.

(JULIET *appears above, at a window.*)

But, soft! What light through yonder window breaks?
It is the East, and Juliet is the sun.
Rise, fair sun, and kill the jealous moon,
Who is sick and pale with grief.
You are more fair than she, and the moon is jealous.
It is my lady. Oh, it is my love!
She speaks, yet she says nothing.
Her eyes speak, but not to me.
Two stars in heaven have business elsewhere,
And ask her eyes to twinkle in their place.

---

1. **rile** stir up; excite

What if her eyes were there, and the stars in her
  head?
The brightness of her cheek would shame those stars,
As sunlight shames a lamp. Her eyes in heaven
Would burn so bright that the birds would sing,
Thinking it day, not night.
See how she places her cheek in her hand!
Oh, that I were a glove on that hand,
That I might touch that cheek!

JULIET: Oh my!

ROMEO: She speaks! Oh, speak again!
  You are as glorious as a heavenly angel.

JULIET: Oh Romeo, Romeo! Wherefore art thou Romeo?[2]
  Deny your father Montague, refuse your name.
  If you will not, swear and be my love,
  And I'll no longer be a Capulet.

ROMEO (*aside*[3]): Shall I hear more, or speak now?

JULIET: It is only your name that is my enemy.
  You are yourself, not just a Montague.
  What's a Montague? Not a hand, a foot,
  An arm, face, or any other part of a man.
  Oh be some other name!
  What's in a name? That which we call a rose
  By any other word would smell as sweet.
  So Romeo would, were he not called Romeo,
  Still have the perfection he owns. Oh, Romeo!
  Drop thy name! Then take all of me.

---

2. **Wherefore art thou Romeo?** Why are you named Romeo?
3. **aside** a term used in plays to indicate that the speaker's
   words are meant to be heard only by the audience and not by
   the other characters in the play.

ROMEO: I take you at your word.
From now on, I will never be Romeo.

JULIET: Who are you that lurks in the night?

ROMEO: I do not know how to tell you who I am.
I hate my name, because it is an enemy to you.
If my name were written, I would tear it up.

JULIET: My ears have heard less than a hundred words
From that mouth, yet I know the voice.
Aren't you Romeo, and a Montague?

ROMEO: Neither, fair lady, if you dislike either one.

JULIET: How did you come here, and why?
The orchard walls are high and hard to climb.
If any of my family find you here, you will die.

ROMEO: I scaled these walls with love's light wings.
Stone walls cannot keep love out.
Love dares to do what it can.
Your family is of no concern to me.

JULIET: If they see you, they will murder you.

ROMEO: There is more danger in your eye
Than twenty of their swords.
Look sweet, and I am ready for their anger.

JULIET: There is nothing in the world I want more
Than for them not to see you.

ROMEO: I have night's cloak to hide me.
But if you don't love me, let them find me here.
It would be better to end my life by their hate,
Than to live without your love.

JULIET: Who told you how to find this place?

ROMEO: Love told me. I am not a ship's pilot,
But if you were a far shore on the farthest sea,

I would sail to find you.

JULIET: The mask of night covers my face,
Or you would see me blush.
You have heard me say too much tonight.
I wish I could pretend to deny it.
Do you love me? I know you will say yes.
But do not swear it, for sometimes lovers lie.
If you do love, say it faithfully.
If you think I am too quickly won over,
I'll frown so that you may charm me more.
But in truth, I am too fond of you to do so.
You may think I'm odd, but trust me.
I'll be more true than those who play hard to get.
I should be more coy, perhaps,
But you have already heard my true feelings.
So please forgive me,
My love is not as light as it might seem.

ROMEO: Lady, I swear by the moon that...

JULIET: Don't swear by the moon,
For it changes month by month.

ROMEO: What shall I swear by?

JULIET: Do not swear at all. If you must,
Swear on yourself and I'll believe you.

ROMEO: By my heart's dear love...

JULIET: Do not swear. Although it makes me happy,
I have no joy about our love tonight.
It is too rash, too sudden.
It is like lightning, which is over
Before one can even say, "Look, lightning!"
Good night, my sweet.
The bud of our love will bloom when next we meet.

ROMEO: Oh, will you leave me so unsatisfied?

JULIET: What satisfaction can you have tonight?

ROMEO: Exchange your faithful vow of love for mine.

JULIET: I gave it to you before you asked for it.
But I will take it back.

ROMEO: Why? For what purpose, my love?

JULIET: To give it to you again.
My love is as deep as the deepest sea;
The more I give, the more I have.
(NURSE *calls offstage.*) I hear someone calling.
In a minute, good Nurse!
Wait here, I will come again. (*She exits.*)

ROMEO: I am afraid this is only a dream.
It is too sweet to be real.

JULIET (*re-enters above*): Three words, dear Romeo,
And then good night. If your love is true,
And your purpose marriage, send me word tomorrow.
I will send someone to you
To ask where and what time we will marry.
Then I'll follow you throughout the world.

NURSE (*offstage*): Madam!

JULIET: I'm coming! (*to* ROMEO) But if you do not want to,
Leave me alone to grieve.
A thousand times good night! (*She exits.*)

ROMEO: It is a thousand times worse
Now that she is gone.

JULIET (*re-enters, above*): Romeo!

ROMEO: My dear?

JULIET: At what time tomorrow
Shall I send the messenger to you?

ROMEO: At the hour of nine.

JULIET: I will not fail. It seems like twenty years
Until then. Oh! I forgot why I called you back.

ROMEO: Let me stand here until you remember.

JULIET: I will forget, with you standing there.
I can only think about how I love your company.

ROMEO: I'll stay, just to have you forget.

JULIET: It is almost morning. I wish you would go,
But no farther than a bird's hop from here.

ROMEO: I wish I were your bird.

JULIET: Sweet, so do I.
But I might kill you with too much love.
Good night, good night! Parting is such sweet sorrow
That I shall say "good night" till it be tomorrow.

(JULIET *exits.*)

ROMEO: Sleep well, and peace in your rest!
Now I must go to Friar Lawrence's cell,
To ask his help, and my happiness to tell.

(ROMEO *exits.*)

Scene 3

Friar Lawrence's cell. FRIAR LAWRENCE *enters with a basket.*

FRIAR: Grey-eyed morning smiles on frowning night,
And tired darkness stumbles away from the fiery
light.
I must fill this basket with weeds and flowers
Before the sun opens his burning eyes.
Great power lies in herbs, plants, and stones.

Nothing living on the earth is so foul
That it does not give us something good.
But there is nothing good that cannot be abused.
Inside this small flower
Lies a strong poison with medical power.
Smelling it will help any sick part,
But tasting it will kill the strongest heart.
In people as well as plants, good and evil lie.
But if the evil is more, the plant will die.

(ROMEO *enters.*)

ROMEO: Good morning, Father.

FRIAR: Bless you!
Who salutes me so sweetly this time of day?
Son, could it be a troubled head
That makes you rise early and leave your bed?
Worries keep old men awake.
Young men sleep well, and dreams they make.
Your being up early tells me something is wrong.
Is this true? Have I hit it right?
Our Romeo has not been to bed tonight.

ROMEO: What you say is true.

FRIAR: My goodness! Were you with Rosaline?

ROMEO: With Rosaline, Friar Lawrence? No.
I have forgotten that name, and that name's woe.

FRIAR: That's good, my son. But where were you, then?

ROMEO: I'll tell you, before you ask me again.
Last night I went to my enemy's dance.
There, Cupid's arrow struck me by chance.
I met my love; we need you now,
To read us both our wedding vows.
A Capulet is she, and I love her so,

We wish to marry, though we both are foes.
I will tell you more later. I hope and pray,
That you will consent to marry us today.

FRIAR: My Goodness! What a change is here!
Is Rosaline, who you did love so dear,
So soon forgotten? Young men's love often lies
Not in their hearts, but in their eyes.
How many tears for Rosaline you shed!
You've wasted them all on a love now dead.
The sun in the sky has yet to clear
The groans you cried in my aging ear.
Have you changed? Oh explain to me then,
Women may fall when there's no strength in men.

ROMEO: You always scolded me for loving Rosaline.
You told me to bury my love.

FRIAR: You have buried one, yet dug up another.

ROMEO: Do not scold me, Friar. The one I love now,
Loves me as well. The other did not.

FRIAR: Come, young man, come now with me.
Your assistant in this I am happy to be.
This marriage may have a happy end.
Let it join your families as married friends.

ROMEO: Oh, let us go. We must do it soon.

FRIAR: Let us be wise, careful, and slow.
They stumble, who too fast go.

(*They exit.*)

Scene 4

A street. MERCUTIO *enters with* BENVOLIO.

MERCUTIO: Where the devil is Romeo?

Didn't he come home last night?

BENVOLIO: Not to his father's house, I hear.

MERCUTIO: That awful Rosaline is still torturing him. He will surely go mad.

BENVOLIO: Tybalt sent a letter to his father's house.

MERCUTIO: I'll bet it's a challenge to a duel.

BENVOLIO: Romeo will answer it.

MERCUTIO: Any man that can write can answer a letter.

BENVOLIO: I mean he will answer the challenge to fight.

MERCUTIO: Poor Romeo! Isn't he already dead? He has been stabbed by Rosaline's looks, shot through the ear by a love song, and had his heart pierced by Cupid's arrow. Is there enough of him left to fight Tybalt?

BENVOLIO: Is Tybalt a threat at all?

MERCUTIO: More a threat than you know. He is an expert swordsman. His rhythm and timing are excellent. He has sliced the buttons off many a good silk shirt. He has been trained in the best fencing[4] schools, and knows all the best moves. Though he is a snob, with fancy clothes and fancy talk, he is still very good with his blade.

(ROMEO *enters.*)

BENVOLIO: Here comes Romeo.

MERCUTIO: He looks very thin, like a dried herring.[5] Flesh, flesh, how you are fishified! Romeo! You tricked us last night.

---

4. **fencing** fighting with swords
5. **herring** a fish

ROMEO: Good morning to you both. What trick?

MERCUTIO: You gave us the slip.[6]

ROMEO: Pardon, good Mercutio, I had business elsewhere. I had no time for manners.

MERCUTIO: That's easy for you to say. Haven't you heard of courtesy?

ROMEO: You mean curtsy? Are you asking me to dance?

MERCUTIO: Get in here, Benvolio. It's too early in the morning for me to be joking.

ROMEO: Can't keep up? I win the match!

MERCUTIO: My! Your wit is very quick and sweet this morning. It is a most sharp sauce. Isn't this better than groaning for love? Now that you are sociable, you are Romeo.

(JULIET'S NURSE *enters with* PETER.)

NURSE: Peter!

PETER: I'm coming!

NURSE: Give me my fan, Peter. Good morning, gentlemen.

MERCUTIO: Good afternoon, fair gentlewoman.

NURSE: Oh! Is it afternoon?

MERCUTIO: I think so. I saw the hands on the clock choking noon dead.

NURSE: Get away from me! What kind of man are you?

ROMEO: A man made to wreck himself.

NURSE: A wreck? I should say so! Gentlemen, can any of you tell me where I may find the young Romeo?

---

6. **You gave us the slip.** You hid from us.

ROMEO: I can tell you. But the young Romeo might be an old Romeo by the time you find him. For better or worse, I think I am he.

NURSE: If you be he, sir, I need to have a private word with you.

BENVOLIO (*laughing, to* MERCUTIO): I think she's going to take him to dinner.

ROMEO: I will go with you.

MERCUTIO: Farewell, ancient lady. Farewell.

(MERCUTIO *and* BENVOLIO *exit.*)

NURSE: My word! I ask you sir, who was that man, that was so full of himself?

ROMEO: A gentleman, Nurse, that loves to hear himself talk.

NURSE: Oh I'll show him! (*to* PETER) Why did you just stand there and let him talk to me like that?

PETER: I saw no harm in what they said. If I had, I would have drawn my weapon. I'll fight any man if there's a reason, and the law is on my side.

NURSE: Coward! (*to* ROMEO) But excuse me, sir. As I told you, my young lady Juliet sent me to find you. But before I tell you what she said, I must tell you something. She is a young and good woman. You had better not be toying with her or leading her on.

ROMEO: Nurse, send this, my regards to your lady. I promise...

NURSE: All right. I will tell her. Oh! She will be a joyful woman.

ROMEO: What will you tell her, Nurse? You are not listening to me.

NURSE: Sir, I will tell her that you promise. Which, as I take it, is an honorable offer.

ROMEO: Tell her to somehow sneak out this afternoon,
And go to Friar Lawrence's cell.
There we will be married.

NURSE: This afternoon, sir? She will be there.

ROMEO: Good Nurse, please wait behind the abbey wall.
In an hour one of my men will bring you
A rope ladder that I will use tonight
To climb secretly to Juliet, my joy.
Keep this a secret, and I'll reward you for your
troubles.

NURSE: Bless you! But can your man keep a secret, too?
Did you ever hear the saying,
"Two can keep a secret, if only one of them knows it"?

ROMEO: I promise you, my man's as true as steel.

NURSE: Well, sir, my lady is the sweetest thing. Oh!
There is a nobleman in town named Paris who is
interested in her. She thinks he is a toad. When I tell
her Paris is as good a man as you, she turns pale in
anger.

ROMEO: Send my regards to your lady.

NURSE: Yes, a thousand times.

(ROMEO *exits.*)

NURSE: Peter!

PETER: What!

NURSE: Peter, take my fan, and let's go.

(*They exit.*)

Scene 5

Capulet's orchard. JULIET *enters.*

JULIET: The clock struck nine when I sent the Nurse.
    She promised to return in half an hour.
    Perhaps she could not meet him? No, that's not it.
    She is slow! Love's messengers should be thoughts,
    Which glide faster than sunbeams,
    As they drive away the darkness over the hills.
    Now the sun has crossed over the highest hill
    Of today's journey. Nine to twelve o'clock
    Is three long hours, yet she still is not here.
    If she had the feelings and warm blood of youth,
    She would fly faster than a thrown ball,
    And my words would be tossed to my sweet love,
    And his, back to me.
    But old people act as if they were dead,
    Clumsy and slow, and heavy as lead.
    Oh good, here she comes!

(NURSE *enters.*)

Oh Nurse, what is the news?
    Have you met with him? Why do you look sad?
    If the news is sad, tell it merrily.
    If it is good, you put it to shame
    By delivering it with a sour face.

NURSE: I am tired. Give me a minute.
    Oh how my bones ache! What a walk I've had!

JULIET: I wish you had my bones, and I had your news.
    Now please, good Nurse, speak.

NURSE: My word, why the rush? Can't you wait?
    Don't you see that I am out of breath?

JULIET: How can you be out of breath,
When you have enough breath to make excuses?
Your excuses are longer than the news.
Is it good or bad?

NURSE: Well, first of all, you do not know how to choose a
man. Why Romeo? His face and legs are better than
all other men's, not to mention the rest of him, but
he's not very polite. He is as gentle as a lamb,
though. Have you had your dinner yet?

JULIET: No, no. What did he say about our marriage?

NURSE: Oh! What a headache I have!
My head could break into twenty pieces.
And my back! My back!
What was in your heart, sending me out and around?
I'll die from all this running up and down!

JULIET: I am sorry that you are not well.
Sweet, sweet Nurse, tell me, what did my love say?

NURSE: Your love says, like an honest, courteous,
Kind, and handsome man... Where is your mother?

JULIET: Where is my mother? She is inside.
Where should she be? What are you saying?
What does he want with my mother?

NURSE: Oh dear! Why are you so mad? Calm down.
Is this how you comfort my aching bones?
From now on, deliver your messages yourself.

JULIET: Such a fuss! Please, what does Romeo say?

NURSE: Can you get out of the house today?

JULIET: Yes.

NURSE: Then you should hurry to Friar Lawrence's cell.
Your husband will be there to make you his wife.
Oh look! Your cheeks turn red with the news!

Get to the church. I must go and get a ladder,
So your love can climb here after it is dark.
I've slaved away for your delight,
But you'll be on your own tonight.
Go! Hurry to the Friar's.

JULIET: I hurry to my happiness. Nurse, farewell.

(*They exit.*)

Scene 6

Friar Lawrence's cell. FRIAR LAWRENCE *enters with*
ROMEO.

FRIAR: Let heaven smile on this holy act.
　　Let sorrow not come to us later!

ROMEO: Whatever sorrow comes, it cannot sour the joy
　　One short minute gives me when I see her.
　　Join our hands with holy words,
　　And let death do whatever he dares.
　　It is enough for me to call her mine.

FRIAR: These violent delights have violent ends,
　　Like when fire and gunpowder meet and kiss.
　　Honey that is too sweet can be sickening.
　　Therefore, love moderately.

(JULIET *enters.*)

JULIET: Good day, Father.

FRIAR: Romeo will thank you for us both.

(ROMEO *kisses her.* JULIET *kisses him back.*)

ROMEO: Juliet, if your joy is like mine,
　　And you can describe it,
　　Fill the air with sweet words.

Sing of the happiness we will receive here today.

JULIET: It is richer than fancy words could ever say.
My true love is so great
That I cannot add it up with words.

FRIAR: Come with me, and we will do our work quickly.
You two cannot be alone
Until the holy church makes you one.

(*They exit.*)

Act 3

Scene 1

A public place. MERCUTIO, BENVOLIO, *and* SERVANTS *enter.*

BENVOLIO: Good Mercutio, let's go home.
   The day is hot and the Capulets are about.
   If we meet, there will probably be a fight.
   These hot days stir up bad blood.

MERCUTIO: You are like one of those fellows who enters a
   tavern and slams his sword on the table. You say "I
   have no need of you, sword!" But by your second
   drink, you are pointing it at the waiter.

BENVOLIO: Am I like that?

MERCUTIO: You are as hot-blooded as anybody, as quick
   to get angry, and as easily annoyed.

BENVOLIO: That too?

MERCUTIO: If there were two of you, we'd soon have none
   of you. One would kill the other. You will quarrel
   with any man just for having more or less hair in his
   beard than you do. Your head is as full of fights as an
   egg has meat. You once argued with a man for
   coughing in the street because he woke your dog.
   Didn't you quarrel with a tailor for wearing his new
   clothes before Easter? You fought another man for
   tying his new shoes with old laces. And you lecture
   me about quarreling!

BENVOLIO: If I were as quarrelsome as you are,
   My life wouldn't be worth a penny.

MERCUTIO: Really? So cheap?

BENVOLIO: By my head, here come the Capulets.

MERCUTIO: By my heel, I do not care.

(TYBALT *and his followers enter.*)

TYBALT: Stay close. I am going to speak to them.
Gentlemen, good day. May I have a word with one of
you?

MERCUTIO: Just a word? Make it a word and a fight.

TYBALT: You will find me ready for one. Just give me a
reason.

MERCUTIO: Can't you find a reason without me giving
you one?

TYBALT: Mercutio, you are one of Romeo's band—

MERCUTIO: Band? What are we, musicians? Just wait
until you hear one our songs! Here's my instrument.
(*He pats his sword.*) This will make you dance!

BENVOLIO: We are in a public place.
You should go somewhere private and argue there.
Here all eyes are watching us.

MERCUTIO: Men's eyes were made to look. Let them
watch.
I will not budge for any man.

(ROMEO *enters.*)

TYBALT: Well, peace be with you, sir.
Here comes my slave now.

MERCUTIO: Your slave? I'll die before
He will ever serve you.

TYBALT: Romeo. You are a villain.

ROMEO: Tybalt, I have my reasons for excusing your
insult.

I see you do not really know me.

TYBALT: Your reasons will not excuse the insults
You have done me. Turn and draw.

ROMEO: I never insulted you.
I like you more than you could ever know.
Until you know why, please calm down.

MERCUTIO: How disgusting! (*He draws his sword.*)
Tybalt, you rat-catcher, will you fight me?

TYBALT: What do you want with me?

MERCUTIO: Just one of your nine lives, kitty!
If need be, I'll cut up the other eight.

(*They fight.*)

ROMEO: Benvolio! Use your sword and knock down theirs.

(ROMEO *steps between them.*)

Gentlemen, stop!
The prince has outlawed fighting in Verona.
Tybalt! Mercutio! Both of you, stop it!

(TYBALT *stabs* MERCUTIO *under* ROMEO'S *arm. He runs off
with his followers.*)

MERCUTIO: I am hurt. I am dying. Where did he go?

BENVOLIO: Are you hurt?

MERCUTIO: It's just a scratch, but enough to kill me.
Where is my servant? Go get a doctor.

(SERVANT *exits.*)

ROMEO: The wound cannot be that bad.

MERCUTIO: It's not as deep as a well, nor as wide as a
church door, but it's enough. If you look for me

tomorrow, you will find me in the grave. I am done for this world. A curse on both your houses! What a cat to scratch a man to death! Why did you come between us? He got me, sneaking under your arm.

ROMEO: I thought it was for the best.

MERCUTIO: Help me into some house, Benvolio.
A curse on both your houses!
They have made worms' meat of me.

(MERCUTIO *and* BENVOLIO *exit.*)

ROMEO: My faithful friend is dying
Because Tybalt insulted me.
Tybalt, my relative of only an hour!
Oh sweet Juliet, your beauty has made me weak.

BENVOLIO (*returning*): Romeo, brave Mercutio is dead!

ROMEO: Today's bad luck will only continue.
It begins a sadness that others must end.

BENVOLIO: Here comes the furious Tybalt again.

(TYBALT *returns.*)

ROMEO: He is alive and Mercutio is dead!
Mercy, away to heaven! Let me be angry now!
Tybalt! Take back your insult!
Mercutio's soul is waiting for you to keep him
company.
Either you or I, or both of us, must join him.

TYBALT: You, wretched boy. You were together on earth.
You will join him again.

(*They fight.* ROMEO *stabs* TYBALT. TYBALT *dies.*)

BENVOLIO: Romeo, run away! People are coming.
Tybalt is dead. Don't just stand there!

The prince will condemn you to death
If you are caught. Leave now!

ROMEO: Oh, I am Fortune's fool!

(ROMEO *exits. The* PRINCE, MONTAGUE, CAPULET, *their*
WIVES, *and others enter.*)

PRINCE: Who started this fight? Where are they?

BENVOLIO: Oh noble Prince, I can tell you what happened
In this fatal brawl.
There lies the man, killed by young Romeo,
Who killed your cousin, brave Mercutio.

PRINCE: Benvolio, who started this?

BENVOLIO: Tybalt, who lies here dead by Romeo's hand.
Romeo tried to speak to him fairly,
Tried to make Tybalt realize
How silly the argument was.
He said you warned against fighting.
But Romeo could not calm him down.
Tybalt's ear was deaf to peaceful words.
He and hotblooded Mercutio fought.
Romeo tried to stop them,
But an evil thrust by Tybalt killed Mercutio
Under Romeo's arm.
Tybalt fled, but then he returned.
Romeo fought for revenge.
Before I could part them, Tybalt fell slain.
As he fell, did Romeo turn and fly.
This is the truth, or let Benvolio die.

LADY CAPULET: He is a Montague,
And his feelings make him lie.
Twenty of them must have fought here,
And twenty of them could kill only one of ours.

Prince, I beg for justice, which you must give.
Romeo slew Tybalt, Romeo must not live.

PRINCE: Romeo slew him, he slew Mercutio. Who must
pay?

MONTAGUE: Not Romeo, Prince. He was Mercutio's friend.
He only ended what the law should have ended—
Tybalt's life.

PRINCE: Though it was Tybalt's fault,
Romeo has committed murder. He must leave Verona.
I have my own interest in this fight.
Mercutio was one of my relatives.
I'll slap all of you with a heavy fine.
Then you'll be sorry for this loss of mine.
No more excuses, by all my power!
If Romeo is found in Verona, that's his last hour!
Take away this body that lies here so still!
Mercy is like murder when it pardons those that kill.

(ALL *exit.*)

Scene 2

Capulet's orchard. JULIET *enters.*

JULIET: Hurry, Sun! Race across the sky
And bring on cloudy night. Close the curtain
Of the evening, so that Romeo
Can come to my arms unseen.
If love is blind, it is best at night.
Come, night! Give me my Romeo.
If he were the stars, he would make heaven so fine
That all the world would be in love with night
And ignore the sun.
I have bought the house of love,

But have not lived in it.
This day is dull and annoying.
I am like a child the night before a party,
That has presents but cannot open them.
Oh, here comes my nurse.

(*Enter* NURSE, *with rope ladder.*)

Now, Nurse, what news? What do you have there?
The ropes that Romeo asked you to get?

NURSE: Yes. (*She throws them down.*)

JULIET: Oh my! What is the news? Why did you do that?

NURSE: He's dead! We are undone, lady!
Pity the day! He's gone, he's killed, he's dead!

JULIET: Could heaven be that envious of us?

NURSE: Romeo can, though heaven cannot. Oh Romeo,
Romeo! Who ever would have thought it? Romeo!

JULIET: Why are you tormenting me?
Has Romeo killed himself?

NURSE: I saw the wound, I saw it with my own eyes.
It was here on his manly chest.
Pity the sight, and all the blood!
I fainted at the sight.

JULIET: Oh, break my heart! Break at once!

NURSE: Oh Tybalt, Tybalt, the best friend I ever had!
I never thought I would live to see you dead!

JULIET: What do you mean, Romeo and Tybalt dead?
My dearest cousin, and my dearer husband?
Trumpets! Sound the end of the world!
Who can live if those two are gone?

NURSE: Tybalt is gone, and Romeo banished.
The Romeo who killed him is banished.

JULIET: Did Romeo spill Tybalt's blood?

NURSE: Curse the day, he did!

JULIET: A snake's heart hidden by a flowery face!
　　Did a dragon ever hide in a cave so well?
　　Evil angel! Wolf-eating lamb!
　　You are just the opposite of what you seemed.
　　Oh, that evil should live in such a gorgeous palace!

NURSE: There's no trust, faith, or honesty in men.
　　They all lie and swear. These sorrows make me old.
　　May shame come to Romeo!

JULIET: Watch your tongue! He was not born to shame.
　　Shame is ashamed to sit on his brow.
　　What a beast I was to speak so badly of him!

NURSE: Will you speak well of your cousin's killer?

JULIET: Should I speak badly of my husband?
　　What words can clear your name,
　　After I, your wife, have ruined it?
　　But why, villain, did you kill my cousin?
　　That villain cousin would have killed my husband.
　　Back, foolish tears, back to your well.
　　Your drops belong to sadness.
　　You make the mistake of falling in joy.
　　My husband lives, who Tybalt would have killed.
　　Tybalt is dead, who would have killed my husband.
　　All this is comfort. Why do I weep then?
　　Tybalt's death was sad enough, if it ended there.
　　But Romeo is banished!
　　Where are my father and my mother, Nurse?

NURSE: Weeping over Tybalt. Do you want to go
　　To them? I will bring you there.

JULIET: They wash his wounds with tears.

When theirs are dry, mine will be used up,
For Romeo.
I will go to my wedding bed.
But not to Romeo. To Death instead.

NURSE: Go to your chamber. I'll find Romeo
To comfort you. I know where he is.
Your Romeo will be here tonight.
I'll go to him. He is hiding in the Friar's cell.

JULIET: Oh, find him! Give him this ring, and beg him
To come here to say his last farewell.

(*They exit.*)

Scene 3

Friar Lawrence's cell. FRIAR LAWRENCE *enters.*

FRIAR: Romeo, come out, you fearful man.
Suffering loves you. You are married to trouble.

(ROMEO *enters.*)

ROMEO: Father, what is the news?
What is the Prince's punishment?
What new sorrow awaits me?

FRIAR: You, my son, are too familiar with bad luck.
The Prince has decided you will not die,
But you will be banished.

ROMEO: Hah, banished! Be merciful, and say "death."
Exile has more terror than death.
Do not say "banished."

FRIAR: From now on, you are banished from Verona.
Be patient. The world is broad and wide.

ROMEO: There is no world outside Verona,
Except torture, and hell itself.

To be banished from Verona
Is to be banished from the world.
And to be exiled from the world is to die.
By calling death banishment,
You cut my head off with a golden axe,
And smile upon the law that murders me.

FRIAR: How ungrateful! The law says you must die,
But the kind Prince took your side.
He changed that awful word "death" to "banishment."
This is mercy, and you do not see it.

ROMEO: It is torture, not mercy. Heaven is here,
Where Juliet lives. Every unworthy thing on earth
Can live here and see her. But Romeo may not.
Even flies can see her, but I must fly.
And you say that exile is not death?
How can you, my friend,
Torture me with that word "banished?"

FRIAR: You are mad.[1] Listen to me!

ROMEO: You will only speak about banishment.

FRIAR: I see that madmen have no ears.

ROMEO: Why should they, when wise men have no eyes?

FRIAR: I must argue with you about your situation.

ROMEO: You cannot speak about what you cannot feel.
If you were as young as I am, and loved Juliet,
Had just married her, killed Tybalt
And been banished, then you might speak.
You would tear your hair, and fall on the ground
As I do now, and think about death.

(*A knock is heard at the door.*)

---

1. **mad** crazy

FRIAR: Rise! Someone knocks. Romeo, hide yourself.

ROMEO: No, I won't.

(*More knocking.*)

FRIAR: Listen! How they knock! Who's there?
Romeo, get up or you will be taken away.
Stand up! Hide in my study.
Who knocks so hard? Where do you come from?
What do you want?

NURSE (*outside*): Let me come in, and you shall know.
I come from Lady Juliet.

FRIAR: Welcome then.

(NURSE *enters.*)

NURSE: Oh, tell me, Father,
Where is my lady's husband? Where's Romeo?

FRIAR: There on the ground, swimming in his own tears.

NURSE: Oh he is just like Juliet!
Just like him, she lies blubbering and weeping.
Stand up and be a man for Juliet's sake!

ROMEO: Nurse! Did you say something about Juliet?
How is she? Does she think I am a murderer?
That I have stained our joy with her cousin's blood?
Where is she? Has she ended our love?

NURSE: She says nothing, sir, but weeps and weeps.
She stops and falls on her bed and then starts up,
And calls for Tybalt, and cries for Romeo,
And then falls down again.

ROMEO: It is as if my name has murdered her,
Just as my hand has murdered her cousin.
Oh tell me, Friar, where in this foul body of mine

Does my name live? Tell me, so I may cut it out.
(*He draws his sword.*)

FRIAR: Hold your desperate hand! Are you a man?
Your shape says you are,
But your tears are like a woman's
And your wildness like a beast's.
You amaze me. I thought you were better tempered.
You have killed Tybalt. Will you kill yourself,
And the lady inside you as well?
Why do you curse your birth, heaven, and earth?
All three meet in you at once,
Which you, at once, would lose.
Your noble shape is but a form of wax.
It lessens the courage of a man.
Like a misbehaved and moody girl,
You pout upon your good fortune and your love.
Go to your wife!
Climb to her chamber and comfort her.
But do not stay too long,
For then you can not go to Mantua.
You will live there until we can find a time
To announce your marriage, reconcile[2] your families,
Beg the pardon of the Prince, and call you back.
Then there will be a thousand times more joy
Than when you left in tears.
Go, Nurse. Ask your lady
To hurry everyone in the house to bed.
Romeo is coming.

NURSE: Here, sir, is a ring she asked me to give you.
Please hurry, for it grows very late.

---

2. **reconcile**   make peace between

(NURSE *exits.*)

ROMEO: How much better I feel!

FRIAR: Go now, and good night. But remember:
　　You must leave before morning,
　　Or by the break of day, in disguise.
　　Go to Mantua. I'll send your servant
　　And he will tell you everything that happens here.
　　It is late. Farewell, and good night.

ROMEO: Farewell.

(*They exit.*)

Scene 4

Capulet's house. CAPULET *enters, followed by* LADY
CAPULET *and* PARIS.

CAPULET: Unlucky things have happened sir,
　　And we haven't had time to tell our daughter.
　　Understand, she loved Tybalt dearly, as did I.
　　Well, we were born to die.
　　It's very late. She'll not come down tonight.
　　I promise you, if you were not here,
　　I would have been in bed an hour ago.

PARIS: These are sad times, and not a time to court.
　　Madam, good night.
　　Speak to your daughter about me.

LADY CAPULET: I will, and will know what she thinks
　　Tomorrow. Tonight she is overwhelmed by grief.

(PARIS *starts to go, but* CAPULET *calls him back.*)

CAPULET: Sir, I'll make a rash offer of my child's love.
　　I think she will obey me. I don't doubt it.
　　Wife, go to her before you go to bed.

Tell her of Paris's love and that this Wednesday...
What day is this?

PARIS: Monday, my lord.

CAPULET: Monday! Well, Wednesday is too soon.
Let it be Thursday. Tell her, Thursday
She will marry this noble man.
We'll make no great ado, just a friend or two.
With Tybalt recently killed,
It may be thought we did not care for our kinsman
If we celebrate too much.
We'll just invite a half dozen friends.
What do you say to Thursday?

PARIS: My Lord, I wish Thursday were tomorrow.

CAPULET: Wife, go to Juliet before you go to bed
And prepare her for her wedding day.
Farewell, my lord.
It is so late that we might call it morning.
Good night.

(*They exit.*)

Scene 5

Capulet's orchard. ROMEO *and* JULIET *enter at the window.*

JULIET: Will you go? It is not yet day.
It was the nightingale, and not the lark,
That sang in your ear.
She sings every night from the pomegranate tree.
Believe me, love, it was the nightingale.

ROMEO: It was the lark, announcing the morning,
Not the nightingale. Streaks of light
Break through the clouds in the east.

The heavenly candles of night have burnt out.
The day stands ready on the misty mountain tops.
I must leave and live, or stay and die.

JULIET: That light is not daylight. It is some meteor
Bearing a torch, lighting your way to Mantua.
Therefore, stay. You do not need to go.

ROMEO: Let me be found here, let me be put to death.
I am content, and will stay to comfort you.
I'll say that the grey light is not morning.
It is only a pale reflection of the moon.
And that is not the lark in the heavens above us.
I have more care to stay than will to go.
Come, death! Juliet wills it so. It is not day.

JULIET: It is day. It is here! Be gone!
It is the lark, singing out of tune.
Some say the lark sings sweetly.
It is not so, for she divides us.
That voice wakes the hunters who will hunt you here.
Romeo, you must leave.
More light comes, and lighter it grows.

ROMEO: More light, and it darkens our woes!

(NURSE *enters.*)

NURSE: Madam!

JULIET: Nurse?

NURSE: Your mother is coming to your chamber.
Daylight has broken. Be careful. (*She exits.*)

JULIET: Window, let the day in, and let life out.

ROMEO: Farewell! One kiss, and I'll descend. (*He climbs down.*)

JULIET: Are you gone? My love, husband, and friend!

I must hear from you every day in the hour,
For in a minute there are many days.
I will be years older before I see my Romeo again.

ROMEO: Farewell! I will take every opportunity
To send my greetings and love to you.

JULIET: Do you think we will ever meet again?

ROMEO: I know we will. And all our tears now
Will be sweet to talk of later.

JULIET: Oh, I see evil ahead! I think I see you below,
As one who is dead in the bottom of a tomb.
Either my eyesight fails, or you look pale.

ROMEO: In my eye, so do you.
Dry sorrow drinks our blood. Farewell to you.

(*He exits.*)

JULIET: Oh Fortune! All men call you fickle.
If you are, what do you need of him?
Be fickle, Fortune.
Do not keep him long, but send him back.

LADY CAPULET (*offstage*): Daughter! Are you up?

JULIET: Who calls? Is it my mother?
Is she going to bed late, or waking early?
What brings her here?

(LADY CAPULET *enters.*)

LADY CAPULET: Juliet! Still weeping for your cousin?
Will you wash him from his grave with tears?
Even if you could, you could not make him live.
Therefore, stop now. Grief shows much of love,
But too much grief shows a lack of sense.
You must be crying so much
Because the villain who killed him still lives.

JULIET: What villain?

LADY CAPULET: That villain Romeo.

JULIET: Yes, madam. If my hands could touch him,
I wish none but I might avenge my cousin's death!

LADY CAPULET: We will have our revenge, do not fear.
Weep no more. I'll send someone to Mantua,
Where that banished runaway lives.
He will give him such strong poison
That he will soon keep Tybalt company.
Then I hope you will be satisfied.

JULIET: I will never be satisfied with Romeo
Until I see him...dead.
If you could find a man to bring the poison,
I would mix it, so Romeo would sleep in peace.
My heart hates to hear him named
And not be able to go to him,
To shower the love I had for my cousin
On the body that slaughtered him!

LADY CAPULET: Find a way, and I'll find such a man.
But now I will tell you something joyful.
You have a careful father. To relieve you
Of your sadness, he has set a day of joy
That you don't expect, nor I looked for.
Early next Thursday morning, the gallant, young,
And noble Paris will make you
A joyful bride at Saint Peter's Church.

JULIET: He cannot make me a joyful bride there.
Why the hurry? Why must I marry someone
Before I am even courted?[3]

---

3. courted to try to gain the love or affection of someone,
especially with hopes of marrying them

Please tell my father that I will not marry.
I'd rather marry Romeo,
Whom you know I hate, than Paris.

LADY CAPULET: Here comes your father.
Tell him yourself and see how he will take it.

(CAPULET *enters with* NURSE.)

CAPULET: When the sun sets, the air drizzles dew.
But for the sunset of Tybalt's life, it rains.
What is it my girl? Still in tears?
Wife, have you told her about our plans?

LADY CAPULET: Yes, but she will have none of it.
Like a fool, she is married to her grave!

CAPULET: She will have none of it? Won't she thank us?
Can't she count her blessings?
Can't she be proud that, though she is unworthy,
We have found such a worthy gentleman to be her
husband?

JULIET: I'm not proud you have done this, only thankful.
I can never be proud of what I hate.
I can only be thankful for what you do in love.

CAPULET: What is this? "Proud," and "thankful"?
Thank me no thankings, nor proud me no prouds.
Prepare your little self for Thursday
To go with Paris to Saint Peter's Church,
Or I will drag you there.
Get out, you pale and sickly little brat!

LADY CAPULET: What are you doing? Are you mad?

JULIET: Good father, I beg on my knees
That you hear me. Let me have just one word.

CAPULET: You disobedient wretch! Get yourself

To church Thursday, or never look me in the face.
Do not answer me. Don't say a word.
Wife, we thought we were blessed
To have only one child.
Now I see this one is too much,
And that we are cursed in having her.

LADY CAPULET: You are too angry.

CAPULET: I have worked too hard all my life
To find her the best husband,
To have her answer, "I'll not wed."
If you will not marry Paris,
You will no longer live in my house.
Thursday is near. Swear you are my daughter,
And I'll marry you to my friend.
Otherwise, beg, starve, and die in the streets.
I will not recognize you, or help you.
Think this over. I will not change my mind.

(*He exits.*)

JULIET: Is there no pity in the clouds
That sees my troubles?
Oh, sweet Mother, do not throw me out!
Delay this marriage for a month, a week.
If you cannot,
Make my bridal bed in the tomb where Tybalt lies.

LADY CAPULET: Don't talk to me. I won't say a word.
Do as you will. I am done with you.

(*She exits.*)

JULIET: Oh Nurse, how will we prevent this?
My husband is on earth, my faith in heaven.
How can I marry when my husband still lives?
Comfort and counsel me.

NURSE: Here are the facts. Romeo is banished.
　　And I say he won't dare come back to claim you.
　　So I think it best you married Paris.
　　Oh, he's a lovely gentleman!
　　Romeo's a dishrag compared to him.
　　I think you will be happy in this second match.
　　It is better than your first.
　　Romeo is as good as dead. You have no use of him.

JULIET: Do you speak from your heart?

NURSE: From my soul too, or curse them both.

JULIET: Amen!

NURSE: What?

JULIET: Well, you are a marvelous comfort to me.
　　Go and tell my mother
　　I have gone to Friar Lawrence's cell,
　　To make confession for disobeying my father.

NURSE: I will. You are wise to do so.

(*She exits.*)

JULIET: Old devil! Oh wicked fiend!
　　You curse Romeo with the same tongue that praised
　　　him.
　　From now on, you and I will separate.
　　I'll ask the Friar for his help.
　　If all else fails, I will seek death myself.

(*She exits.*)

Act 4

Scene 1

Friar Lawrence's cell. FRIAR LAWRENCE *enters with* PARIS.

FRIAR: You wish to marry this Thursday, sir?
   That is too soon.

PARIS: Capulet wants it so
   And I don't want to slow him down.

FRIAR: You say you do not know what Juliet thinks of this.
   This is wrong. I do not like it.

PARIS: She is still weeping over Tybalt's death,
   So I have talked little about love.
   Love does not smile in a house of tears.
   Her father thinks it is dangerous
   That she is still mourning,
   And has rushed our marriage to stop her tears.
   That is why we hurry.

FRIAR (*aside*): I wish I did not know why.
   Look, sir, here comes Juliet.

(JULIET *enters.*)

PARIS: I am happy to see you, my lady and my wife!
   Have you come to confess to the Friar?

JULIET: To answer you would be to confess to you.

PARIS: Do not deny to him that you love me.

JULIET: I will confess to you that I love him.

PARIS: So will you, I am sure, say that you love me.

JULIET: If I do, it would be worth more
   To say it behind your back than to your face.

PARIS: Poor soul, your face has been abused by tears.
That face is mine, and you have damaged it.

JULIET: That may be so, for it is not mine to give.
Are you free now, Friar?
Or shall I come to you later tonight?

FRIAR: I am free now, my daughter.
Paris, Juliet and I must talk in private.

PARIS: I would not dare intrude.
Juliet, on Thursday I will come for you early.
Until then, farewell. I blow you a kiss.

(*He exits.*)

JULIET: Oh, shut the door, Father! Come weep with me!

FRIAR: Ah, Juliet, I already know your problem
And it troubles me more than I can bear.
I hear you must marry Paris on Thursday,
And nothing can delay it.

JULIET: Do not tell me what you have heard
Unless you can tell me how to prevent it.
If you cannot help me, I'll kill myself.
You joined mine and Romeo's hearts and hands
together.
If you join me to another, you will kill that union.
As you have lived long and have much wisdom,
Please give me some advice now.
If you cannot, a bloody knife will do. Speak.
I long to die if you cannot offer me a remedy.

FRIAR: Hold on, daughter. I see a hopeful solution,
Though it is as desperate as yours.
Since you have the courage to kill yourself,
You will likely try something like death,
Rather than marry Paris.

If you dare to do that, I'll give you the remedy.

JULIET: I'd rather leap off a tower than marry Paris.
I'd walk with thieves, and lurk with snakes.
Chain me to a bear, lock me in a tomb, and cover me
    with bones.
I would do all these without fear or doubt,
Rather than stain my marriage to my sweet love.

FRIAR: All right. Go home, be merry, and agree
To marry Paris. Wednesday is tomorrow.
That night, make sure you are alone in your chamber.
When you are in bed, take this bottle
And drink the medicine inside.
A cold and drowsy feeling
Will run through your veins,
And your heart will almost stop.
No warmth from your body or breath will say you are
    still alive.
The rose color in your lips and cheeks will fade
To pale ashes. Your eyes' windows will close,
Like death when he shuts up the day of life.
Your body will appear stiff, stark, and cold,
As if you were dead.
You will stay like this for forty-two hours.
Then you will wake, as if from a pleasant sleep.
When Paris comes in the morning to wake you,
You will appear dead.
As is the custom in our country,
They will dress you in your best robes
And carry you to the ancient tomb
Where all the Capulets lie.
In the meantime, while you sleep,
I will write to Romeo of our plan,
And he will come here.

He and I will be there when you wake,
And Romeo will take you to Mantua.
This will free you from your problem,
Unless you are afraid to do it.

JULIET: Give it to me! Do not tell me about fear!

(*The* FRIAR *hands her the bottle.*)

FRIAR: Patience. Go home and be strong.
I'll send someone to Mantua
With a letter for your husband.

JULIET: Love give me strength, and strength help me.
Farewell, dear father!

(*They exit.*)

Scene 2

A hall in Capulet's house. CAPULET, LADY CAPULET,
NURSE, *and two* SERVANTS *enter.*

CAPULET: We have invited many guests. They are written
here.

(*He gives a list to* FIRST SERVANT, *who exits. He addresses
the* SECOND SERVANT.)

Sir, go and hire me twenty good cooks.

SECOND SERVANT: You will not have any bad ones, sir. I
will only hire the good ones, those that can lick their
fingers.

CAPULET: How can you tell by that?

SECOND SERVANT: Simple, sir. A bad cook will not lick his
own fingers. Therefore, whoever cannot lick his
fingers will not be hired.

CAPULET: Go, be gone.

(SECOND SERVANT *exits.*)

> We are unprepared for this wedding.
> Has my daughter gone to Friar Lawrence?

NURSE: Yes, sir.

CAPULET: Hopefully he will do some good for her,
> That silly, good-for-nothing girl.

NURSE: Here she comes, with a merry look.

(JULIET *enters.*)

CAPULET: Now, my stubborn child! Where have you been?

JULIET: I am sorry for disobeying you.
> Friar Lawrence told me to fall before you
> And beg your pardon.

(*She falls on her knees.*)

> Pardon, I beg you! From now on I will obey you.

CAPULET: Send for Paris and tell him this.
> They will marry tomorrow morning!

JULIET: I met him at Lawrence's cell,
> And gave him what love I could
> Without crossing the line of modesty.

CAPULET: I am glad. Stand up.
> This is as it should be.
> Let me see Paris. Bring him here.
> Our city has much to thank that Friar for.

JULIET: Nurse, will you go with me to my room
> And help me sort the special clothes
> I need for tomorrow?

(JULIET *and* NURSE *exit.*)

LADY CAPULET: Tomorrow? We will be short of supplies.
It is now near night!

CAPULET: Don't worry. All will be well, I promise you.
Go to Juliet and help her prepare.
I won't go to bed tonight.
I'll play the housewife for once.
Oh, all the servants are gone!
Well, I'll go to Paris and prepare him
For tomorrow. My heart is light.
Our wayward girl has come back to us.

(*They exit.*)

Scene 3

Juliet's room. JULIET *enters with* NURSE.

JULIET: Yes, those clothes are best.
Nurse, please leave me alone tonight.
I must pray for heaven to smile upon my situation,
Which is miserable and full of sin.

(LADY CAPULET *enters.*)

LADY CAPULET: Do you need my help?

JULIET: No, madam. We have taken care of everything
Necessary for tomorrow. Please leave me alone now
And let the nurse stay up with you tonight.
I am sure you have your hands full
With all this sudden business.

LADY CAPULET: Good night. Go to bed. You must rest.

(LADY CAPULET *and* NURSE *exit.*)

JULIET: Farewell! God knows when we shall meet again.
A fearful chill runs through my veins.

It freezes life's heat.
Perhaps I'll call them back to comfort me.
Nurse! No. What could she do here?
I must do this alone. (*holds potion*) Come, bottle.
What if this potion does not work at all?
Will I have to marry tomorrow morning?
No. This will prevent it. Lie yourself there.

(*She lays a dagger beside her.*)

What if the Friar gave me poison,
To hide his shame for marrying me to Romeo?
I fear it is, and yet I know it isn't.
He is a holy man.
What if, when I am laid in the tomb,
I wake before Romeo can come for me?
Will I breathe the foul air and die,
Before my Romeo comes?
Even if I live, it will be like death
To stay in a dark tomb where, for many hundred years,
The bones of all my buried ancestors are placed.
Where bloody Tybalt, just laid in the earth,
Lies rotting in his burial gown.
They say night spirits live down there,
And when the living hear them, they go crazy.
No, it is not true!
But won't I go just as crazy with fear?
Will I go mad, and pluck a bone from the grave
And club out my desperate brain?
Oh, look! I think I see my cousin's ghost
Seeking Romeo, whose sword killed him.
Stay Tybalt, stay! Romeo I come to you!
I drink this for you!

(*She drinks the potion and falls upon her bed.*)

Scene 4

A hall in Capulet's house. LADY CAPULET *enters with* NURSE.

LADY CAPULET: Fetch more spices, nurse.

NURSE: They call for dates in the pastry, too.

(CAPULET *enters.*)

CAPULET: Come! Stir! The rooster has crowed,
    It is three o'clock. Take care of the baked meats.

NURSE: Get out of here, you house-husband!
    Get to bed. You'll be sick tomorrow
    For staying up so late.

CAPULET: I have stayed up all night before,
    And have never been sick.

(LADY CAPULET *and* NURSE *exit.* SERVANTS *enter with logs and baskets.*)

What do you have there?

FIRST SERVANT: Things for the cook, sir, but I don't know what.

CAPULET: Hurry then!

(*First Servant exits.*)

Boy, fetch drier logs for the fire.
Call Peter. He will show you where they are.

SECOND SERVANT: I am smart enough to find them.
    I don't need to bother Peter for that.

(*He exits.*)

CAPULET: Good point!
    Goodness! It is day! Paris will soon be here,

With the musicians. I hear him coming.

(*Music is heard.*)

Nurse! Go wake Juliet and dress her up.
I'll go and chat with Paris. Hurry, I say!

(ALL *exit.*)

Scene 5

Juliet's room. NURSE *enters.*

NURSE: Juliet! She is fast asleep I think.
Wake up sleepy-head! What, not a word?
Sleep a little now, sleep for a week later.
My, how soundly she sleeps! I must wake her up.
Madam! What? You are dressed and in your clothes!
I must wake you. Lady! Lady! Oh no!
Help! My lady's dead! Oh, curse the day I was born!
My lord! My lady!

(LADY CAPULET *enters.*)

LADY CAPULET: What is all this noise? What is the matter?

NURSE: Look, look! What a terrible day!

LADY CAPULET: Oh no! My child, my only life.
Wake up or I will die with you!
Help, help! Call for help.

(CAPULET *enters.*)

CAPULET: For shame, bring Juliet out. The groom is here.

NURSE *and* LADY CAPULET: She's dead! She's dead! Oh
curse the day!

CAPULET: Let me see her. Oh no! She's cold.
Her blood is settled and her joints are stiff.

The life has long left her lips.
Death lies on her, like frost upon the sweetest flower.

NURSE *and* LADY CAPULET: Oh sorrowful day! Oh sad
times!

CAPULET: Death has taken her away to make me cry.
It ties up my tongue, and will not let me speak.

(FRIAR LAWRENCE *enters with* PARIS *and* MUSICIANS.)

FRIAR: Is the bride ready to go to church?

CAPULET: Ready to go, but never to return.
Paris, my son! Death has married your wife
The night before your wedding day.
There she lies, a flower picked by him.
Death is my son-in-law. Death is my heir.

PARIS: Have I waited all morning just to see this?

LADY CAPULET: Accursed, unhappy, hateful day!
The worst hour Time has ever seen!
Our poor child, our one joy,
Cruel death has taken her from my sight!

NURSE: It is the saddest day I have ever seen!
Never was there such a day as dark as this!

PARIS: I am tricked and divorced by you, death!
You are cruel! Oh love! Oh life!

CAPULET: Time! Why did you come now to kill our joy?
Oh child! You are dead! My child is dead.
With her, my joys are buried.

FRIAR: Be still! For shame! The cure
For this disaster is not more confusion.
Heaven and you had a part of Juliet.
Now heaven has it all,
And the better it is for her.

You wanted to see her move ahead in life.
That was to be your heaven.
Now you cry, seeing that she
Has moved on to heaven itself?
Dry your tears, and lay flowers
On her fair body.
Dress her in her finest robes and bring her to church.
Remember, though now we cry,
Where she's gone, she's happier than you or I.

CAPULET: All the things that we had for a wedding
Are now for a funeral.
Our instruments change to crying bells.
Our wedding is now a sad burial feast.
Our bridal flowers will now decorate her tomb.
Everything must now be changed to the opposite.

FRIAR: Sir and madam, go in.
And you, Paris. Everyone!
Follow Juliet as we carry her to her grave.
Heaven has punished your sins with pain,
Obey God's laws, so you won't be punished again.

(*Exit* ALL *but* MUSICIANS *and* NURSE.)

FIRST MUSICIAN: Let us pack up our pipes, and go.

NURSE: Yes, put away your instruments.
As you have seen, this is a sorry case.

(*She exits.*)

FIRST MUSICIAN (*holding up his broken pipe case*): Yes,
though I think the case can be mended.

(PETER *enters.*)

PETER: Musicians! Make me feel better and play "Heart's
ease."

FIRST MUSICIAN: Why "Heart's ease"?

PETER: Because my heart plays "My heart is full of woe."
Oh, play me some merry tune to comfort me.

FIRST MUSICIAN: No. It is no time to play now.

PETER: I will find something to give you.

FIRST MUSICIAN: Oh? What will you give us?

PETER: Not money. How about this dagger?

SECOND MUSICIAN: Hey! Put that away!

PETER: I will stab you with my wit instead! Explain
something to me, musicians. It is said:
"When sadness wounds the heart,
And sad songs hurt your mind,
Turn to music with her silver sound..."
Now why is it "silver sound"?

FIRST MUSICIAN: Because silver has a sweet sound?

PETER: What do you say?

SECOND MUSICIAN: I say "silver sound" because
musicians play for silver.

PETER: And you?

THIRD MUSICIAN: I don't know what to say.

PETER: It is "music with her silver sound" because
musicians never get any gold for sounding.[1] Hah!

(*He exits.*)

FIRST MUSICIAN: What a strange person he is!

SECOND MUSICIAN: Forget him. Let's go in here. We'll
wait for the mourners, and stay for dinner.

(*They exit.*)

---

1. **sounding** playing (making sounds with their instruments)

Act 5

Scene 1

Mantua. A street. ROMEO *enters.*

ROMEO: If I can trust my dreams, they say joyful news is
    coming.
    My heart is light. All day a happy spirit
    Lifts me above the ground. It was a strange dream.
    My lady came and found me dead.
    She kissed the life back into me. I was a king!
    Ah! How sweet is love when its dreams are so rich!

(BALTHASAR *enters.*)

    News from Verona! Hello, Balthasar!
    Do you have letters from the Friar?
    Is my father well? How is my Juliet?
    Nothing can be ill, if she is well.

BALTHASAR: Then she is well, and nothing is ill.
    Her body sleeps and her soul is with the angels.
    I saw her laid in the tomb,
    And came here to tell you.

ROMEO: Is this true? Then I defy you, stars!
    Hire a horse. I will leave here tonight!

BALTHASAR: Please sir, have patience.
    You look pale and wild. Do not leave like this.
    It could be dangerous.

ROMEO: No, you are wrong. Do what I asked you to do.
    You don't have a letter for me from the Friar?

BALTHASAR: No, sir.

ROMEO: It doesn't matter. Go and get the horses.

I'll be with you soon.

(BALTHASAR *exits.*)

Juliet, I will lie beside you tonight.
How shall I do it? Ah! I do remember a druggist
Who lives around here.
He had tattered clothes,
And looked like a starving beggar.
His shop was a mess and run down.
I remember thinking that if anyone sold poison
In Mantua, it would be that wretched man.
How was I to know I would need it?
Here is the building. Hello? Druggist!

(DRUGGIST *enters.*)

DRUGGIST: Who is yelling?

ROMEO: Come here. I see you are hungry and poor.
Here's forty gold coins. Sell me a bottle of poison.
Something that will cause the breath of life
To leave the body as fast as gunpowder fires a cannon.

DRUGGIST: I have such deadly drugs, but Mantua's law
Means death for anyone who sells or talks about
them.

ROMEO: Are you afraid to die? You look dead already.
The world is not your friend, nor are its laws.
There is no law that can make you rich,
So don't be poor. Break the law and take the money.

DRUGGIST: If I weren't poor, I would not do this.
I do this against my will.

(*He gives* ROMEO *the poison.*)

ROMEO: I'm paying your poverty, not your will.

DRUGGIST: Pour this in any liquid and drink it.
Even if you have the strength of twenty men,
It will kill you.

ROMEO: Here is your gold. Money murders more
Than all the poisons you could sell.
Farewell. Buy food, and make yourself well.
This is wine, not poison.
Now, I take you
To Juliet's grave. There I drink this magic dew.

(*They exit.*)

Scene 2

Friar Lawrence's cell. FRIAR JOHN *enters.*

FRIAR JOHN: Hello? Brother Lawrence?

(FRIAR LAWRENCE *enters.*)

FRIAR: That sounds like Friar John.
Welcome back from Mantua! What did Romeo say?
Do you have a letter from him?

FRIAR JOHN: No. Before I left, I went to find
Another brother to come with me.
I found him in a house visiting the sick.
The health inspectors thought the house
Was infected by the plague,[1]
So they locked us in and would not let us leave.
I was not able to go to Mantua.

FRIAR: Who took my letter to Romeo?

---

1. **plague** a serious, easily caught disease that strikes many people at the same time. In 1347–1351, an outbreak of bubonic plague (also called "Black Death") killed 25 million people in Europe.

FRIAR JOHN: I still have it here.
I could find no messenger to bring it.
They were all afraid of the plague.

FRIAR: Oh no! That letter was of great importance.
By not sending it, we may cause much danger!
Friar John, go and get me a crowbar.[2]

FRIAR JOHN: Brother, I'll go and bring it to you.

(FRIAR JOHN *exits.*)

FRIAR: Now I must go to the tomb alone.
In three hours, Juliet will wake.
She will be angry that Romeo
Was not told of our plan.
But I will write to Mantua again
And hide her until Romeo comes.
Poor living girl, closed in a dead man's tomb!

(*He exits.*)

Scene 3

A churchyard with a tomb belonging to the Capulets.
PARIS *enters with his* SERVANT, *who carries flowers and a torch.*

PARIS: Give me your torch and stand there.
No, put the torch out. I do not want to be seen.
Wait over there by those trees.
If you hear anyone coming, whistle to me.
Give me those flowers. Do as I say. Go.

SERVANT (*aside*): I am scared to stand alone

---

2. **crowbar** a bar of iron or steel used to pry open or move heavy objects

Here in the churchyard. Still, I will go.

(*He exits.*)

PARIS: Sweet flower. I lay flowers on your burial bed.
How sad! Your blankets are dust and stones.
Every night I will come to your grave,
And water your flowers with my tears.
(*Servant whistles.*) Someone is coming!
What wretch sneaks in here tonight,
Disturbing my love's sleep?
Night! Hide me. (*He hides.*)

(ROMEO *enters with* BALTHASAR, *who carries a torch and tools.*)

ROMEO: Give me the axe and a crowbar.
Here, take this letter to my father early in the
morning.
Give me the light. Now swear upon your life.
Whatever you hear or see,
Stand back and do not interrupt me.
I am opening this death bed to see my lady's face.
I must take a precious ring from her dead finger.
I need it to live. Now go!
If you try to peek at what else I intend to do,
I will tear you limb from limb
And scatter your parts all over this churchyard.

BALTHASAR: I will go sir, and not trouble you.

ROMEO: You show me true friendship.
Live, prosper, and farewell, good fellow.

BALTHASAR (*aside*): All the same, I'll hide nearby.
The way he looks, I doubt his plans. (*He hides.*)

ROMEO: You awful tomb, you womb of death.

You have gorged yourself
With the dearest morsel of the earth.
Open your rotten jaws!
I'll cram you with more food!

(*He opens the tomb.*)

PARIS: It is that banished Montague,
Who murdered my love's cousin,
And caused her to weep to death.
He has come to do shame to the dead.
I will stop him. (*Steps forward.*) Stop, evil Montague!
Can you take more revenge on the dead?
Condemned[3] villain, I arrest you.
Come with me. You must die.

ROMEO: Indeed I must die. That is why I came here.
Good sir, do not tempt a desperate man.
Fly from here and leave me.
I beg you, do not force me to sin again. Be gone!
I value your life more than mine.
I have come armed against myself.
Do not stay. Go away and live.
Say that a madman's mercy made you run away.

PARIS: I will ignore your nonsense.
I arrest you for being an outlaw here.

ROMEO: Will you provoke me? Then fight!

(*They fight.*)

SERVANT: Oh no! They are fighting! I will call the guard.
(SERVANT *exits.*)

PARIS: Oh, I am slain! (*He falls.*) If you are merciful,

---

3. **condemned** guilty

Open the tomb and lay me with Juliet. (*He dies.*)

ROMEO: I promise I will. Let me see your face.
Mercutio's relative! The noble Paris!
What did Balthasar say as we rode from Mantua?
I think he said Paris was going to marry Juliet.
Did he say that? Or did I dream it?
Or was I crazy, hearing him talk of Juliet,
To think it was true?
Give me your hand, Paris.
We have both written in the book of bad luck!
I'll bury you in a magnificent grave.
A grave? Oh no! Here lies Juliet.
Her beauty makes this grave a hall full of light.
Death, lie there yourself, buried by another dead man.

(*He lays* PARIS *in the tomb.*)

Oh my love, my wife!
Death, who sucked the honey of your breath,
Has not stolen your beauty.
It still lives in your lips and cheeks.
Tybalt! Is that you there in your bloody sheet?
Oh, what better favor can I do you
Than to kill the one who cut your youth in two?
Forgive me, cousin! Ah, dear Juliet.
Why are you still so beautiful? Does death
Love you too, and keep you in the dark as his bride?
For fear of that, I will stay with you,
And never leave this palace of night again.
Here I will stay with the worms that are your maids.
Here I will set up my everlasting rest,
And break heaven's hold on this weary body.
Eyes, take your last look! Arms, your last embrace!
Lips, the doors of breath,

Kiss and seal my bargain with death!
Come, bitter poison!
Pilot my sick and weary ship onto the rocks! Here's
    to my love! (*He drinks the poison.*)
Honest druggist, your poison is fast.
A kiss, and I die, with Juliet at last. (*He dies.*)

(FRIAR LAWRENCE *enters with his tools.*)

FRIAR: By the saints, I must hurry! Oh! Who's there?

BALTHASAR: A friend, Father, who knows you well.

FRIAR: Bless you!
    Tell me, my good friend, what torch is over there
    That lends its light to grubs[4] and eyeless skulls?
    I see it comes from the Capulets' tomb.

BALTHASAR: It does, sir. My master is there.

FRIAR: Who is it?

BALTHASAR: Romeo.

FRIAR: How long has he been there?

BALTHASAR: For half an hour.

FRIAR: Come with me to the tomb.

BALTHASAR: I wouldn't dare, sir.
    He said he would kill me if I did.

FRIAR: Stay, then. I'll go alone.
    I fear something terrible has happened.

BALTHASAR: As I slept under this tree,
    I dreamt my master and another fought,
    And that my master killed him.

FRIAR: Romeo! What blood is this,

---

4. **grubs** the wormlike form many insects have when they are
newly hatched

Which stains the stony door of this tomb?
Why do these bloody swords lie here in this place of
  peace?

(*He enters the tomb.*)

Romeo! You are pale. What? Paris too,
Covered in blood? What an unkind hour!
The lady moves.

JULIET (*waking up*): Oh Friar! Where is my lord?
Where is my Romeo?

(*Noise is heard offstage.*)

FRIAR: I hear a noise. Lady, we must leave this nest
Of death and unnatural sleep.
A greater power than we can defy
Has ruined our plans. Come away.
There your husband lies dead, and Paris, too.
Come, I'll hide you in a sisterhood of holy nuns.
Do not stay to ask why. The guard is coming.
Come and go, good Juliet. I do not dare stay here any
  longer.

JULIET: Go, get away. I will not leave.

(FRIAR *exits.*)

What's this? A cup closed in my true love's hand?
Poison, I see, has killed him.
Romeo! You drank it all, and did not leave
A friendly drop for me?
I will kiss your lips.
Perhaps some poison hangs on them to kill me, too.
(*She kisses him.*) Your lips are still warm!

FIRST WATCHMAN (*offstage*): Lead on. Which way?

JULIET: Noise? I'll be brief. Oh happy dagger!

(*She takes* ROMEO'S *dagger.*)
This is your sheath.[5] (*She stabs herself.*)
Rust there and let me die.
(*She falls on* ROMEO'S *body, and dies.*)

(PARIS'S SERVANT *enters with* WATCHMEN.)

SERVANT: This is the place. There, where the torch burns.

FIRST WATCHMAN: The ground is bloody. Search the
   churchyard.
Go, some of you, and catch whoever you can.
Pitiful sight! Here lies Paris dead,
And Juliet bleeding, still warm, newly dead.
She was buried here just two days ago.
Go tell the Prince! Run to the Capulets!
Wake up the Montagues!

(*Some of the* WATCHMEN *return, with* BALTHASAR.)

SECOND WATCHMAN: Here's Romeo's servant.
   We found him in the churchyard.

FIRST WATCHMAN: Hold him until the Prince comes.

(*Other* WATCHMEN *return, with* FRIAR LAWRENCE.)

THIRD WATCHMAN: Here is a friar that trembles, sighs,
   And weeps. We took these tools from him
   As he was leaving the churchyard.

FIRST WATCHMAN: This is strange. Hold the Friar, too.

(PRINCE ESCALUS *enters, with the* CAPULETS *and others.*)

PRINCE: What can go wrong this early in the morning?

CAPULET: What is it that makes the people scream?

---

5. sheath   a case for the blade of a knife or dagger

LADY CAPULET: The people in the street cry Romeo,
  Some Juliet, and some Paris.

PRINCE: What is going on?

FIRST WATCHMAN: Here lies the noble Paris, dead.
  And Romeo dead. And Juliet, dead before,
  Still warm and newly killed.

PRINCE: Find out how these murders happened.

FIRST WATCHMAN: Here is a friar, and Romeo's servant.
  We found them with tools to open tombs.

CAPULET: Oh, wife! Look how our daughter bleeds!
  This is a Montague's dagger in my daughter's heart!
  It should be in Romeo's back!

LADY CAPULET: Oh my! This sight of death is a bell
  That signals my own death.

(MONTAGUE *and others enter.*)

PRINCE: Come, Montague, see your son and heir.

MONTAGUE: Prince, my wife died last night.
  Grief over Romeo's banishment stopped her breath.
  Can more sadness plot against my old age?

PRINCE: Look, and you will see.

MONTAGUE: Romeo! What manners did I teach you,
  To have you go to the grave before your father?

PRINCE: Let us not cry anymore
  Until we can figure out what happened.
  Then I will rule upon this sadness,
  Even if it means that more must die.
  Meanwhile, be patient. Bring out the suspects.

FRIAR: I know what has happened here.

PRINCE: Then say what you know.

FRIAR: Romeo, lying there dead, was Juliet's husband.
　　Juliet, there dead, was Romeo's faithful wife.
　　I married them, and their secret marriage day
　　Was Tybalt's doomsday. Tybalt's death
　　Banished the newly made groom from the city,
　　And Juliet cried for him, not her cousin.
　　To stop her weeping,
　　Lord Capulet planned to have Juliet marry Paris.
　　She came to me, looking wild, and begged me
　　To stop this second marriage,
　　Or she would kill herself in my cell.
　　I gave her a sleeping potion
　　That would make her appear dead.
　　Then I wrote to Romeo, to come back tonight
　　And take her from her borrowed grave
　　When the potion wore off.
　　But the person I sent could not deliver the letter.
　　When it was time for her to wake,
　　I came alone to the tomb to take her and hide her
　　Until I could send for Romeo.
　　But when I came, a few minutes before she woke,
　　I found Romeo and Paris lying here dead.
　　She then woke up, and I begged her to leave.
　　Then a noise scared me from the tomb
　　And she did not come with me.
　　It seems she did this violence to herself.
　　This is what I know.
　　And the Nurse also knows of the marriage.
　　If this is all my fault, I surrender my life.
　　Take it before its time, according to the law.

PRINCE: We still think of you as a holy man.
　　Where's Romeo's servant? What can he say about this?

BALTHASAR: I brought my master news of Juliet's death.

Then he hurried from Mantua
To this same place, to this tomb.
He asked me to give this letter to his father,
And threatened to kill me if I went into the tomb.

PRINCE: Give me the letter. I will look at it.
Where is Paris's servant, who called for the guards?
Why was your master here?

SERVANT: He came with flowers for his lady's grave.
He asked me to stand back, so I did.
Then someone came with a light to open the tomb.
My master drew his sword on him,
And then I ran away for help.

PRINCE: Romeo's letter agrees with the Friar's words.
It talks about his love, and Juliet's death.
Here he writes that he bought poison from a druggist,
And came to this tomb to die and lie with Juliet.
Where are the enemies? Capulet! Montague!
See what your hate has done.
Heaven tried to kill your anger with love.
By allowing your feud, I, too, have lost two of my
    family.
We are all punished.

CAPULET: Brother Montague, give me your hand.
Let a handshake be your wedding gift to my daughter.
I can ask no more.

MONTAGUE: But I can give you more.
I will build a statue of her in pure gold.
As long as Verona's name is known,
There will be no one as valued
As the true and faithful Juliet.

CAPULET: I will do the same for Romeo,
And have him lie beside her.

Poor sacrifices of our hate!

PRINCE: A gloomy peace the morning brings.
The sun, in sorrow, will not show his head.
Go now and talk of these sad things.
Some will be pardoned, some punished instead.
For never was a story more full of woe
Than this of Juliet and her Romeo.

(ALL *exit.*)

SUMMARY OF THE PLAY

ACT 1

Servants of the Capulets see servants of the Montagues on the street. They fight. Prince Escalus says that anyone else who fights will be put to death. Romeo tells Benvolio why he is unhappy. He loves Rosaline, but she does not love him. Benvolio tells Romeo to find another woman. Romeo answers that he can love only Rosaline.

Count Paris asks Capulet if he can marry Juliet. Capulet invites Paris to a party he is giving that night. Capulet's servant cannot read the list of guests. He asks Romeo to read the list to him. Benvolio suggests that he and Romeo go to the party. He wants Romeo to meet other women.

Lady Capulet tells Juliet that Paris wants to marry her. The guests arrive for the party.

Romeo and his friends are on their way to the party. Romeo is still thinking about Rosaline. He talks about a bad dream he had last night. Mercutio teases Romeo for believing in dreams.

Romeo sees Juliet and forgets Rosaline. Juliet's cousin, Tybalt, recognizes Romeo's voice. He wants to fight with him. Capulet forbids Tybalt to fight at the party. Romeo and Juliet meet. They fall in love. As the party ends, they discover that their families are enemies.

ACT 2

After the party, Romeo slips away from Benvolio and Mercutio. He goes into the Capulet garden.

Romeo watches Juliet at her window. She talks to herself. She says how much she loves Romeo. She wishes that he were not a Montague. Romeo and Juliet declare their love for each other. Juliet says she will send a messenger to Romeo tomorrow, to see if he will marry her.

Romeo tells Friar Lawrence that he no longer loves Rosaline. He wants to marry Juliet. The Friar agrees to marry them. He hopes this marriage will end the feud.

Benvolio and Mercutio meet Romeo on the street. Juliet's nurse arrives. Romeo sends word to Juliet that she should sneak away that afternoon and go to Friar Lawrence's cell. They will be married there.

Juliet waits for the nurse to return. At first the nurse talks only about how tired she is. She finally tells Juliet that Romeo will marry her.

Juliet meets Romeo at the Friar's cell. The Friar leads them out to be married.

ACT 3

Mercutio, Benvolio, and Romeo encounter Tybalt and other Capulets. Tybalt insults Romeo, but Romeo will not fight. Mercutio and Tybalt fight. Romeo tries to stop them. Tybalt kills Mercutio, then runs away. When Tybalt returns, he and Romeo fight. Romeo kills Tybalt. The Prince decides that Romeo will not be put to death, but he must leave Verona.

The Nurse tells Juliet what has happened. Juliet is upset that her cousin is dead, but is glad that her husband is alive.

Friar Lawrence tells Romeo that he has been banished. The Nurse arrives and tells them how upset Juliet is. The Friar tells Romeo to go to Juliet, but warns that he must leave Verona by morning.

Capulet tells Paris that he may marry Juliet. The wedding day is set for Thursday.

It is the next morning. Romeo and Juliet say good-bye. Romeo leaves for Mantua. Lady Capulet tells Juliet that she is to marry Paris. Juliet refuses. Capulet says that if she does not obey him, he will throw her out of his house.

ACT 4

Juliet goes to the Friar for help. He gives her a sleeping potion that will make her appear to be dead. She will be placed in the Capulet tomb. The Friar and Romeo will be at the tomb when she wakes up. Then Romeo and Juliet can run away together.

Juliet apologizes to her father and agrees to marry Paris. Capulet decides the wedding will be tomorrow.

Juliet takes the potion.

The next morning, everyone thinks Juliet is dead. The Friar says she must be placed in the Capulet tomb.

ACT 5

Romeo's servant brings word that Juliet is dead. Romeo decides to go to Verona. He will kill himself so he can be with Juliet. He buys poison from a druggist.

Friar Lawrence is told that Romeo did not receive his letter. The letter explains what really happened to Juliet. The Friar hurries to the Capulet tomb so he will be there when Juliet wakes up.

Paris goes to the tomb. Romeo arrives. They fight, and Romeo kills Paris. Romeo believes Juliet is dead, and takes the poison. The Friar arrives, and Juliet wakes up. Hearing a noise, the Friar runs away. Juliet sees that Romeo is dead, and kills herself. The Prince, Capulet, and Montague arrive. The Friar tells them what happened. Montague and Capulet end their feud and say they will build gold statues of Romeo and Juliet.

REVIEWING YOUR READING

ACT 1

FINDING THE MAIN IDEA

1. Romeo meets Juliet at

    (A) the Capulet party (B) the Montague party (C) the Prince's palace (D) Paris's home.

REMEMBERING DETAILS

2. Tybalt is Romeo's

    (A) cousin (B) servant (C) enemy (D) brother.

3. Benvolio is Romeo's

    (A) cousin (B) servant (C) enemy (D) brother.

4. Mercutio wants Romeo to go the party to

    (A) meet Juliet (B) meet Rosaline (C) forget Juliet (D) forget Rosaline.

5. The penalty for fighting in the streets of Verona is

    (A) jail (B) banishment (C) a fine (D) death.

6. Queen Mab is

    (A) the Prince's mother (B) a fairy who causes dreams
    (C) Romeo's mother (D) Juliet's mother.

7. Tybalt recognizes Romeo by his

    (A) voice (B) face (C) walk (D) laugh.

8. Lady Capulet compares Paris to

    (A) a book (B) a lion (C) a fire (D) a lamp.

DRAWING CONCLUSIONS

9. Juliet is upset when she learns Romeo is a Montague because
    (A) Rosaline is in love with a Montague (B) her family and the Montagues are bitter enemies (C) Montague owes her father money (D) Capulet promised the Prince he would never invite a Montague to one of his parties.

10. Tybalt is angered by Romeo's presence at the party because Romeo

(A) won't dance   (B) is a Capulet   (C) is a Montague   (D) loves Rosaline.

USING YOUR REASON

11. Capulet commands Tybalt not to fight Romeo because

(A) he likes Romeo   (B) Romeo loves Juliet   (C) Tybalt will ruin the party   (D) it is against the law.

IDENTIFYING THE MOOD

12. The constant feuding between the Montagues and the Capulets creates a feeling of

(A) happiness   (B) anger   (C) sadness   (D) tension.

THINKING IT OVER

13. What does the Nurse think about Paris? How do you think this will affect her relationship with Juliet?

14. Why does Capulet ask Paris to come to the party? What does this say about his relationship with Juliet?

ACT 2

FINDING THE MAIN IDEA

1. What is the most important event in this act?

(A) Romeo and Juliet plan to marry.   (B) Friar Lawrence cautions Romeo about love.   (C) Mercutio insults the Nurse.   (D) The Nurse delivers a message.

REMEMBERING DETAILS

2. The Nurse thinks Romeo is

(A) crazy   (B) rude   (C) smart   (D) strong.

3. The morning after the party, the Friar thinks Romeo

(A) has been with Rosaline   (B) has been with Juliet   (C) has slept in the woods   (D) has fought with the Capulets.

4. Mercutio thinks Tybalt is

(A) a good swordsman   (B) an easy opponent   (C) a friend   (D) a coward.

5. Mercutio thinks that Tybalt's letter to Romeo is probably
   (A) an insult (B) a challenge (C) a complaint (D) an apology.

6. When the Nurse delivers Romeo's message to Juliet, Juliet looks
   (A) happy (B) tired (C) angry (D) worried.

7. When Romeo first sees Juliet in her room, he compares her to
   (A) the moon (B) the earth (C) the sun (D) a bird.

DRAWING CONCLUSIONS

8. Juliet fears that she might be telling Romeo she loves him too
   quickly because
   (A) they barely know each other (B) her father will be angry
   (C) Rosaline will be jealous (D) Romeo might think she doesn't
   really mean it.

9. The Friar is at first concerned about Romeo's
   (A) love for Juliet (B) sudden change of love (C) presence at
   Capulet's party (D) not sleeping well.

IDENTIFYING THE MOOD

10. After Romeo meets Juliet, he is
    (A) clever (B) serious (C) angry (D) no different.

THINKING IT OVER

11. Juliet wishes Romeo would change his name. Why? *because his enemy*

12. Juliet does not want Romeo to swear by the moon that he loves
    her. Why? *it changes month by month*

13. What does Friar Lawrence mean when he says "violent delights
    have violent ends"? What do you think this will have to do with
    what happens in the play? *Something that is to good can turn up bad.*

ACT 3

FINDING THE MAIN IDEA

1. What is the most important event in this act?
   (A) Mercutio dies. (B) Juliet visits Friar Lawrence. (C) Romeo
   kills Tybalt. (D) Mercutio warns Benvolio about his temper.

REMEMBERING DETAILS

2. Tybalt calls Romeo a
    (A) villain   (B) farmer   (C) criminal   (D) lamb.

3. Mercutio is killed by
    (A) Romeo   (B) Benvolio   (C) Tybalt   (D) Juliet.

4. When the Nurse tells Juliet that someone has been killed, who does Juliet first think it is?
    (A) Romeo   (B) Tybalt   (C) Benvolio   (D) Capulet

5. Juliet cries for
    (A) Romeo   (B) Tybalt   (C) A and B   (D) none of the above.

6. Capulet finally decides that Paris will marry Juliet on
    (A) Wednesday   (B) Thursday   (C) Friday   (D) Sunday.

DRAWING CONCLUSIONS

7. Mercutio becomes angry with Romeo because
    (A) he won't fight   (B) he loves Rosaline   (C) he disappeared the night before   (D) he jokes too much.

8. Romeo is sentenced to banishment rather than death because
    (A) he is innocent   (B) the Prince likes him   (C) the true blame is too hard to determine   (D) he has already run away.

USING YOUR REASON

9. Romeo thinks his love for Juliet has made him weak because
    (A) now he's happy   (B) he no longer wants to be with his friends   (C) he no longer wants to fight with the Capulets   (D) he is now afraid to die.

10. Why would Juliet rather hear the nightingale than the lark?
    (A) The lark has an ugly voice.   (B) The lark sings when it is morning.   (C) The nightingale reminds her of Romeo.   (D) The lark will wake her father.

11. By the end of this act, Juliet has changed her feelings about
    (A) the Nurse   (B) Tybalt   (C) Romeo   (D) her father.

IDENTIFYING THE MOOD

12. What word best describes Juliet's reaction to the killings?

    (A) anger (B) sadness (C) confusion (D) all of the above

13. Mercutio can best be described as

    (A) hotblooded (B) calm (C) nervous (D) unhappy.

14. Who is angriest when Juliet refuses to marry Paris?

    (A) Lady Capulet (B) Capulet (C) Paris (D) the Nurse

THINKING IT OVER

15. Why does Romeo hate banishment so much? Why does Friar
    Lawrence get angry at Romeo for his reaction to being banished?

16. Juliet tells her mother that she wants to kill Romeo herself. Why
    does she say this?

ACT 4

FINDING THE MAIN IDEA

1. If you were to summarize this act, which title would be the best?
   (A) Paris Gets His Wish (B) The Secret Plan (C) The Capulets
   Plan a Party (D) Capulet's Woe

REMEMBERING DETAILS

2. Juliet goes to the Friar
   (A) to make confession (B) to ask his help (C) to see Paris
   (D) to pray.

3. Whose idea is it to use the sleeping potion?
   (A) Juliet's (B) the Friar's (C) Romeo's (D) the Nurse's

4. The potion will last
   (A) 24 hours (B) 42 hours (C) 48 hours (D) 12 hours.

5. Which of the following people do not know about the potion?
   (A) Romeo (B) the Friar (C) Juliet (D) none of the above

6. What does Juliet fear the most about the tomb?
   (A) ghosts (B) She might suffocate. (C) She might go crazy
   with fear. (D) all of the above

7. Who does Juliet see right before she drinks the potion?

(A) the Friar   (B) the Nurse   (C) Tybalt's ghost   (D) her mother

THINKING IT OVER

8. The sleeping potion is dangerous, but Friar Lawrence gives it to Juliet anyway. What do you think of the Friar's plan?

9. How would you describe Juliet's feelings when she is about to take the potion?

10. Why do you think Shakespeare ends this act with the musicians? What purpose does it serve?

ACT 5

FINDING THE MAIN IDEA

1. Which title seems the most appropriate for this act?

(A) Everybody Dies   (B) Peace at Last   (C) A Bitter Peace
(D) Children's Revenge

REMEMBERING DETAILS

2. When he is banished, Romeo lives in

(A) Mantua   (B) Verona   (C) Padua   (D) Venice.

3. What word best describes the druggist?

(A) old   (B) uncaring   (C) desperate   (D) wealthy

4. Friar John could not deliver the letter to Romeo because

(A) he left it at home   (B) he was locked in a house because of the plague   (C) Friar Lawrence forgot to give it to him
(D) he lost it.

5. Paris visits Juliet's tomb to

(A) see if she is inside   (B) keep others out   (C) lay flowers on her grave   (D) kill himself.

6. Romeo visits Juliet's tomb to

(A) see if she is inside   (B) keep others out   (C) lay flowers on her grave   (D) kill himself.

7. Romeo orders Balthasar to deliver a letter to

(A) Montague   (B) Capulet   (C) the Prince   (D) Friar Lawrence.

8. Who sees Romeo and Paris fight?

    (A) Balthasar   (B) Paris's servant   (C) A and B   (D) none of the above

9. Who calls the guard?

    (A) Balthasar   (B) Paris's servant   (C) A and B   (D) none of the above

10. Juliet kills herself with

    (A) Romeo's poison   (B) her father's sword   (C) Paris's dagger
    (D) Romeo's dagger.

11. By the end of the play, Lady Montague is

    (A) dead   (B) angry at Romeo   (C) crying for Juliet   (D) angry at Lady Capulet.

12. Who will build statues to Romeo and Juliet?

    (A) Capulet   (B) Montague   (C) A and B   (D) none of the above

DRAWING CONCLUSIONS

13. Why does Romeo lay Paris in the Capulet tomb?

    (A) Paris is a Capulet.   (B) Paris asks to be laid next to Juliet.
    (C) He wants to hide the body.   (D) Paris's tomb isn't ready yet.

14. Juliet will not leave the tomb with the Friar because

    (A) she cannot move   (B) she is upset about Romeo   (C) she is still asleep   (D) she is afraid of a noise.

USING YOUR REASON

15. Why does the druggist give Romeo the poison?

    (A) He needs the money.   (B) It is his job.   (C) He likes Romeo.
    (D) He does not know it is poison.

16. At the end of the play, who does the Prince think has been punished?

    (A) the Friar   (B) Balthasar   (C) Paris   (D) everyone

IDENTIFYING THE MOOD

17. What words best describe the mood when the play ends?

    (A) happy and hopeful   (B) angry and violent   (C) sad and regretful   (D) tense and suspicious

THINKING IT OVER

18. Who is Paris related to? How does this make Romeo feel when he kills him? What does this have to do with the rest of the play?

19. If you were the Prince, whom would you punish for Romeo's and Juliet's deaths? Why?

20. What did Friar Lawrence hope Romeo and Juliet's marriage would do for the Capulets and Montagues? With this in mind, comment about the end of the play.